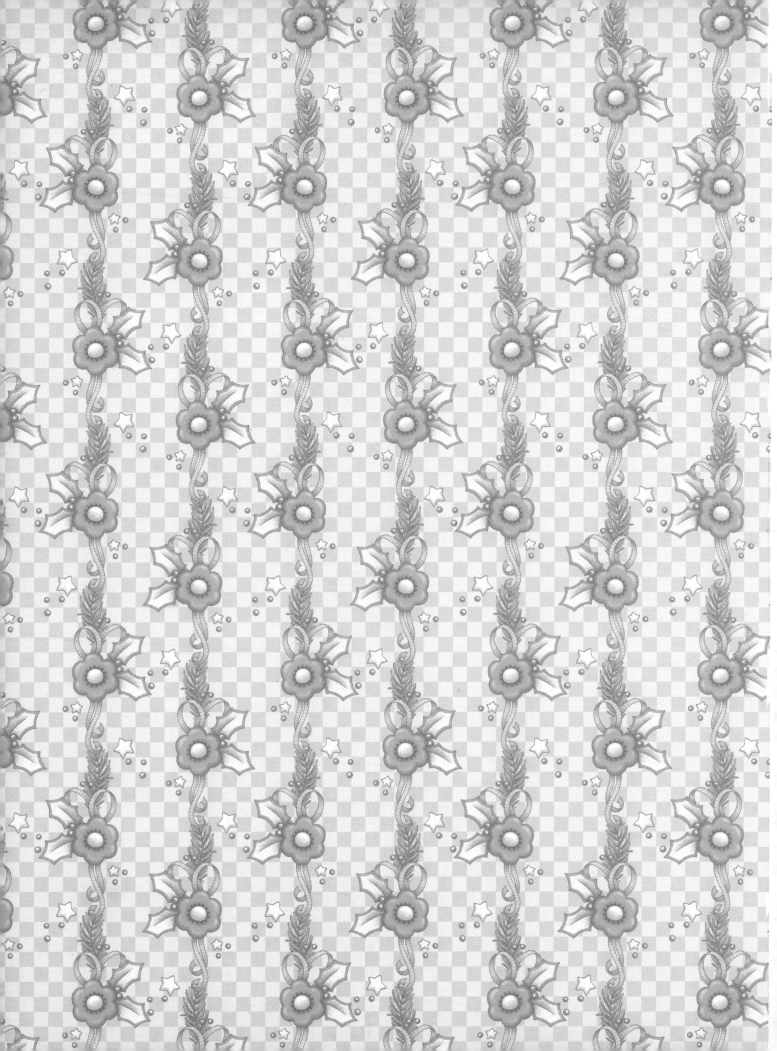

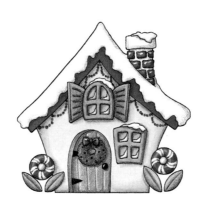

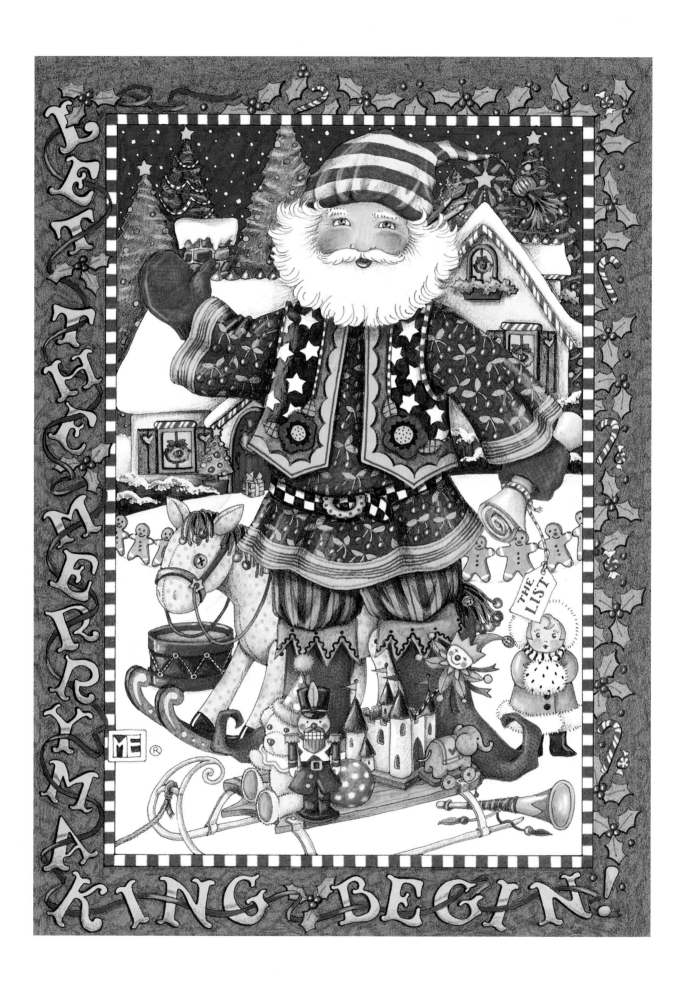

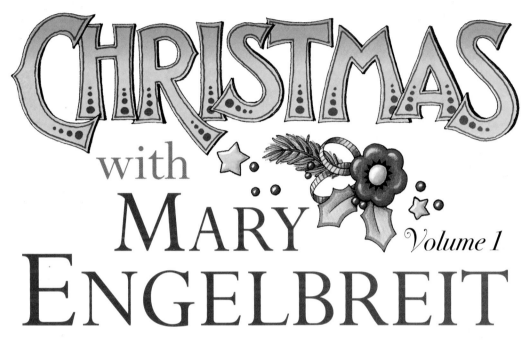

CHRISTMAS
with
MARY
ENGELBREIT

Volume 1

LET THE MERRYMAKING BEGIN

Illustrated by *Mary Engelbreit*

Written by *Virginia Carey*

**Andrews McMeel
Publishing**

Kansas City

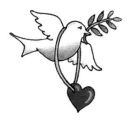

The publishers gratefully acknowledge permission to reproduce the photographs by
Cheryl Dalton, Eric Johnson, Jenifer Jordan, and Barbara Elliott Martin, which originally
appeared in *Mary Engelbreit's Home Companion* magazine, © Universal Engelbreit Cox.
See Photography Credits on page 143 for further information.

Published simultaneously by Andrews McMeel Publishing and Oxmoor House, Inc.

www.andrewsmcmeel.com
www.maryengelbreit.com

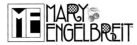

 is a registered trademark of Mary Engelbreit Enterprises, Inc.

Library of Congress Cataloging-in-Publication Data
Engelbreit, Mary.
     Christmas with Mary Engelbreit : let the merrymaking begin /
     illustrated by Mary Engelbreit.
           p. cm. — (Christmas with Mary Engelbreit ; vol. 1)
     ISBN 0-7407-1870-3
       1. Christmas decorations. 2. Christmas cookery. 3. Handicraft.
       I. Title.
    TT900.C4 E52 2001
    745.594'12—dc21   2001045189

First U.S. Edition
01 02 03 04 05 MHN 10 9 8 7 6 5 4 3 2 1

Produced by Smallwood & Stewart, Inc., New York City
Recipe developer: Sarah Zwiebach

ATTENTION: SCHOOLS AND BUSINESSES
Andrews McMeel books are available at quantity discounts with bulk purchase for educational,
business, or sales promotional use. For information, please write to: Special Sales Department,
Andrews McMeel Publishing, 4520 Main Street, Kansas City, Missouri 64111.

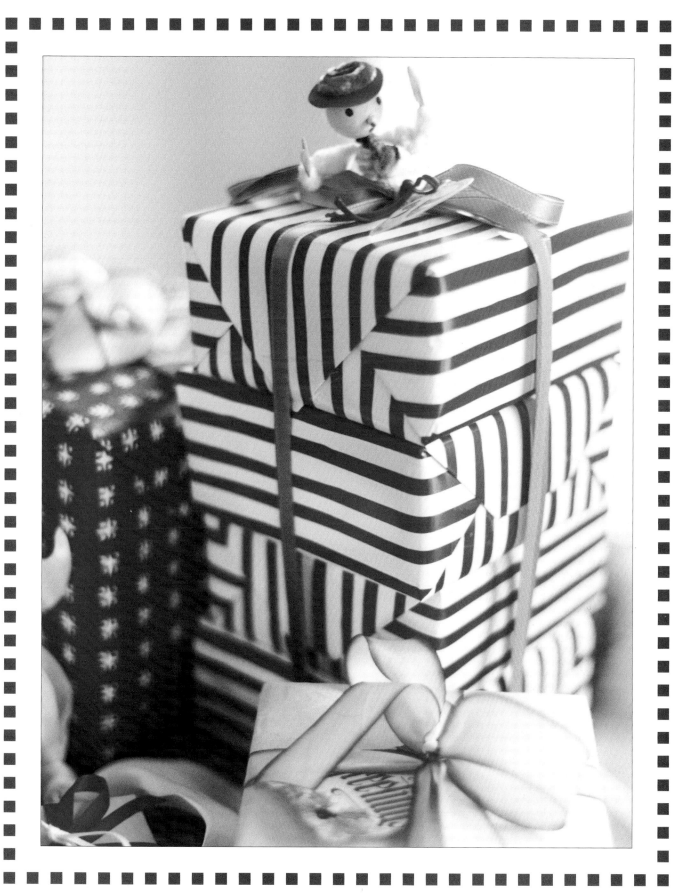

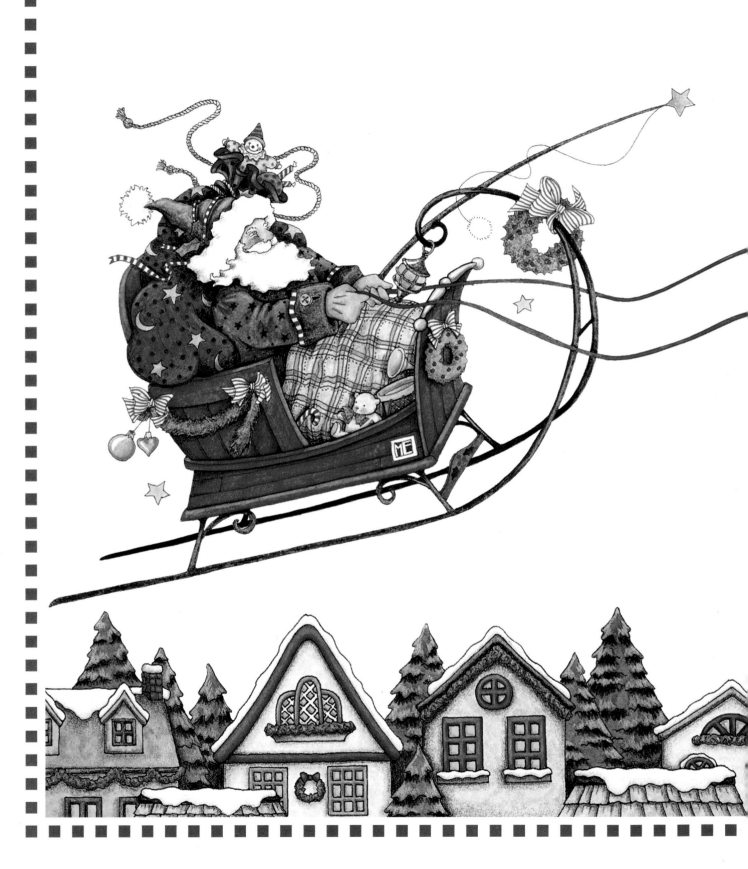

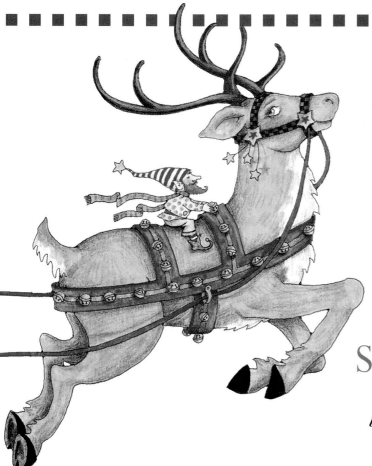

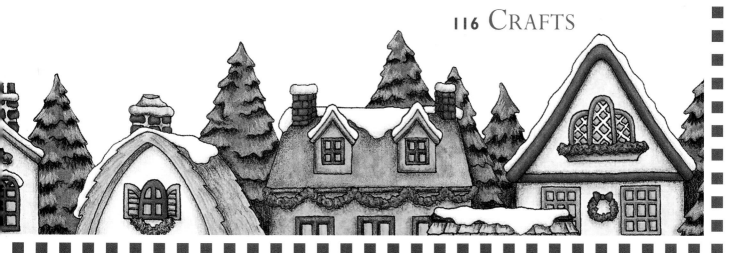

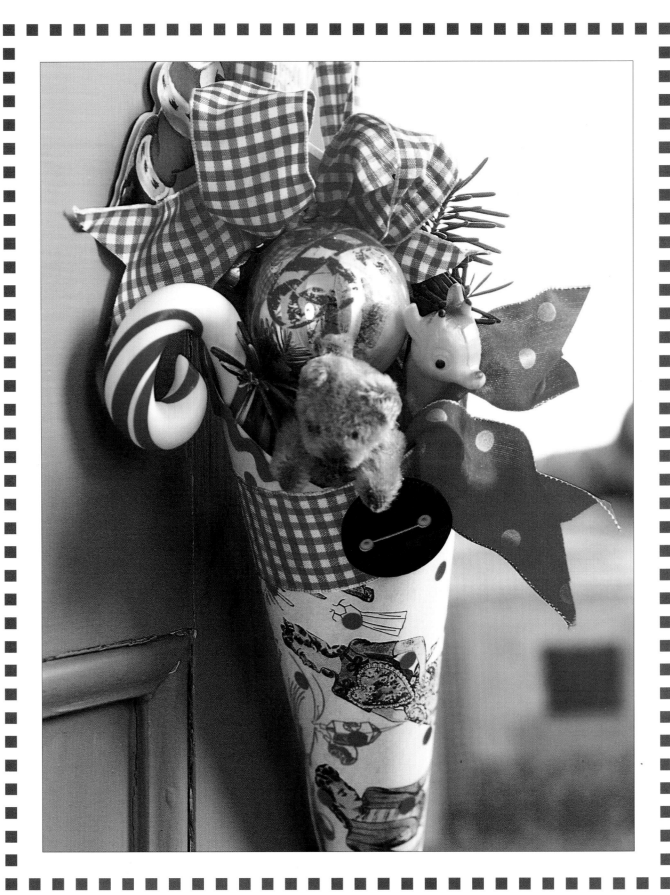

*H*olidays are the high points on my calendar, and none so high as Christmas. Unlike Independence Day or Thanksgiving, Christmas is a season unto itself, with weeks full of joyous celebrations. Oh, yes, there are the endless activities: making lists, writing cards, shopping, wrapping, decorating, entertaining. Somehow, though, even in the cold snap of December, I see these not as obligations but as blessings. We are so fortunate that Christmas arrives to lift us out of our daily lives for just a bit, to connect us with our loved ones. In this book, I want to share with you the best of my Christmases, from the ones I remember as a young girl to this year's celebration. I hope you will find inspiration in these pages to make your holiday a happy one. Merry Christmas!

Mary Engelbreit

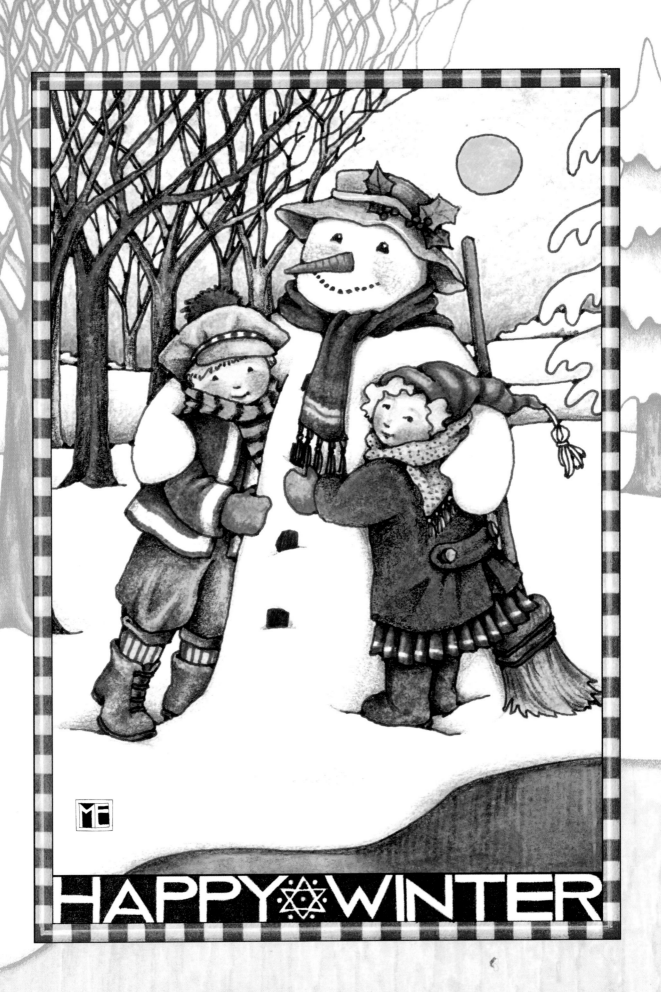

HAPPY✡WINTER

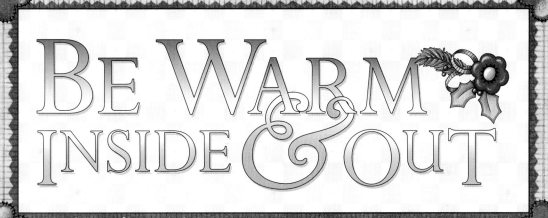

BE WARM
INSIDE & OUT

Center your
celebration on
the magic of
the outdoors—
it's a natural!

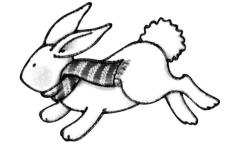

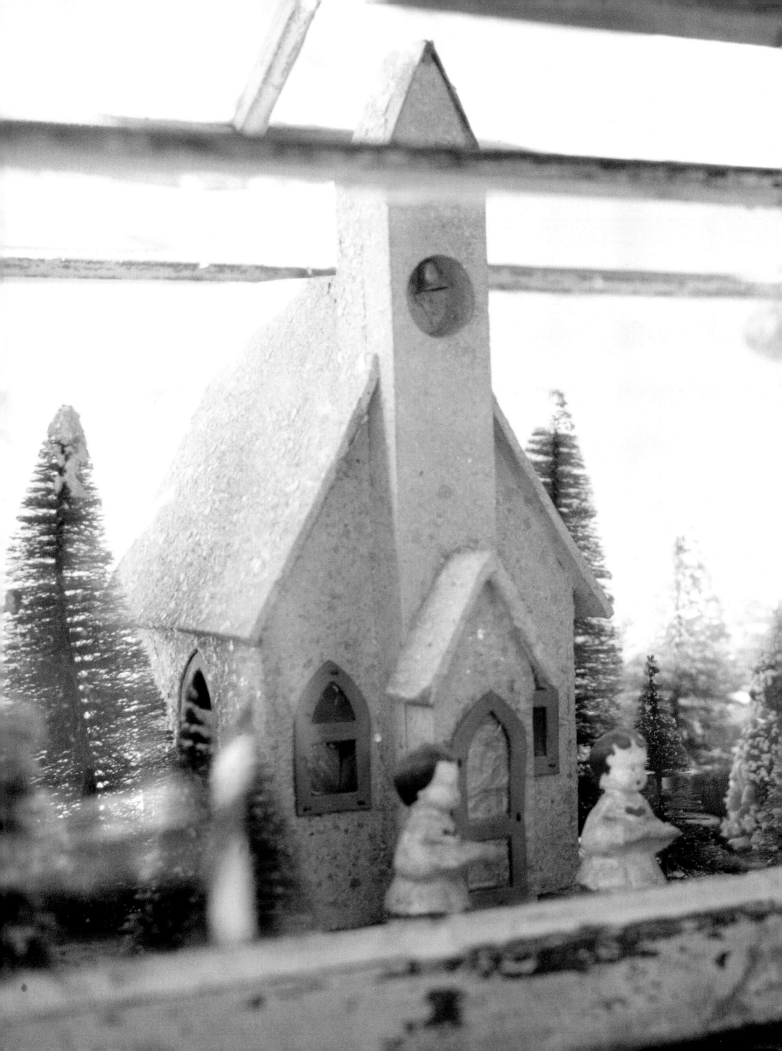

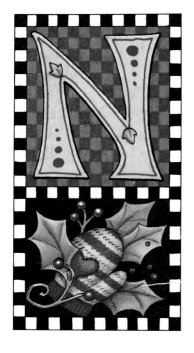

ature creates so many Christmas gifts. Consider the tree that yesterday stood shivering outside but today brings such warmth and beauty to your living room. Look at the pinecone—it fits right into your palm. Breathe in the crisp fragrance of spruce. Twirl around in the fantasia of the first snowfall. That's part of the magic of Christmas. Once the ice is thick enough, you lace up your skates, just as you have every winter. Snow skis, toboggans, and sleds carry the thrills of childhood. Welcome Nature into your home for the holidays—she's a delightful guest, engaging and cordial to visitors of all ages. She'll bring to the festivities a modest and demure spirit you won't find anywhere else.

Nature Sends out Her Season's Greetings

THE HOLLY LEAF AND the sprig of winterberry are more beautiful when they're brought indoors. The colors of the season aren't just limited to poinsettia red and dark green: Pine boughs can be like blue ice; eucalyptus berries, almost lavender; juniper berries, a sweet teal. Bringing Nature to the celebration soothes the transition from outdoors to in—plus it's fast and inexpensive. Who could ask for more?

When the owner of this home plans her annual holiday decorations, she thinks in terms of the whole house, almost as if she's casting a big play. There is the star: the enormous tree festooned with petite, delicate pale-colored ornaments that are in perfect proportion to its graceful branches. Vintage garlands of glass beads lead the eye from one bauble to the next, so that the gazer is continuously drawn into the character of the tree. Clear glass lights create a glow that rivals candlelight. And there are supporting players. A slender topiary couple preen in urns, their stems dressed in ivory ribbons. Above the mirror, a sassy bouquet of dried peapods is tied with the same ivory ribbon, there to be admired with each glance at the looking glass. In the sunroom, buckets of creamy variegated holly hang securely from both doors of the armoire; conifer valances laze across the windows. If some bit of greenery is not just the right shade, it's lightly sprayed with silver paint to soften its tone. Why not let these natural decorations stage a celebration

CHRISTMAS CORNER

A tree doesn't have to monopolize the room, dictating that furniture be removed and foot traffic patterns reconfigured. A ceiling-high tree snuggled into a corner makes it possible to pile presents underneath, knowing they won't be accidentally trampled. Here, the colors of the tree and its ornaments—gentle green and pale golds—echo the home's everyday palette: a cream white for walls and seating furniture, natural wood for chests and mirrors, gilt on birdcages, and soft greens in fabrics. The ornaments' tones play right along in harmony.

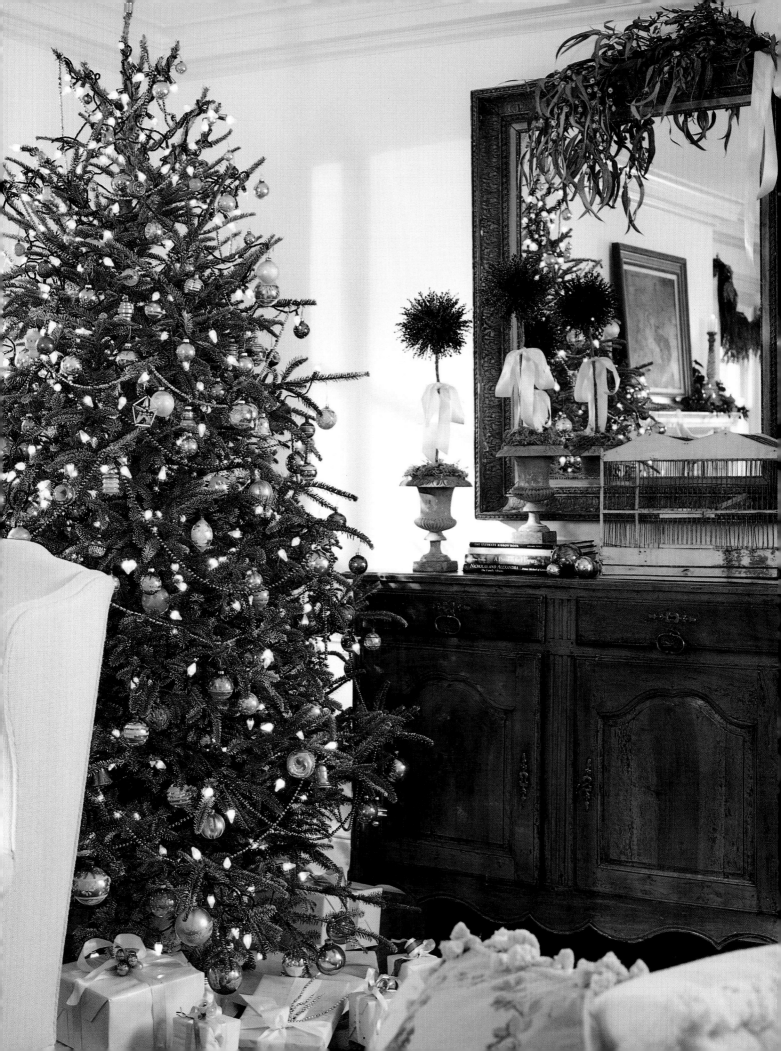

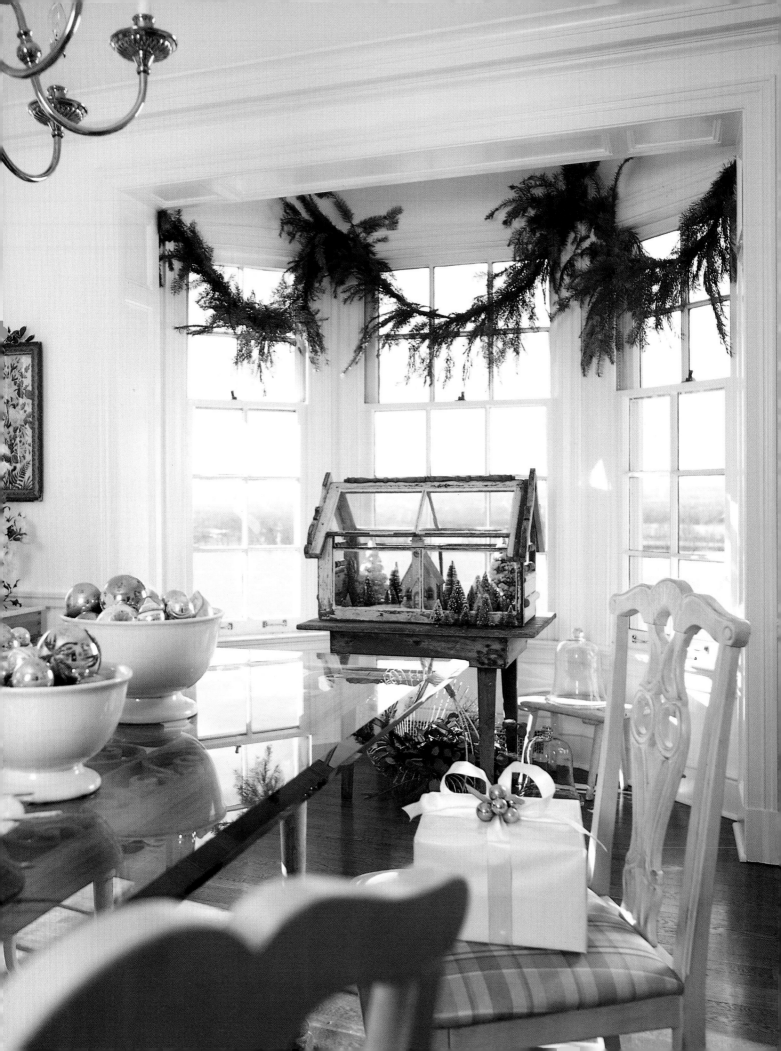

in your house? They are sure to add humor, charm, and surprise.

Think about pulling your collections together in new ways. Antique toys are as much about Christmas present as they are about childhood past. Delight visitors by dressing toys in the holiday spirit. Or create a gnome-size forest of bottle-brush trees and nestle it in a glass case.

Take advantage of the greens and whites of forced bulbs; paperwhites are especially failproof. Pot them in interesting containers, gather their stems in those leftover strands of ribbon or lace, and voilà: decorations that can be a favor for a favorite guest, a hostess gift, or even a perfect present for that somebody you meant to add to your list.

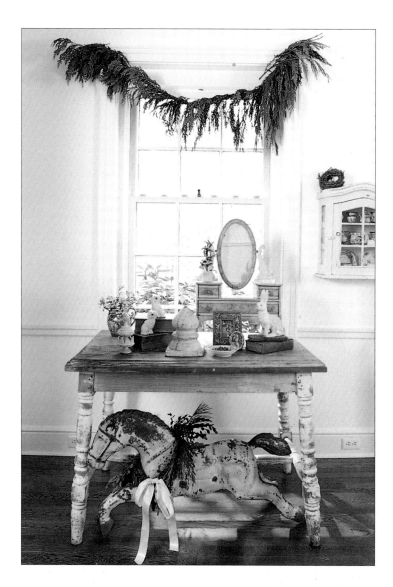

THROUGH THE FOREST, A HOLIDAY CHURCH

Taking over favorite everyday items and interpreting them for Christmas is a popular technique for adding whimsy to every room. This adorable greenhouse, made of salvaged windows, takes pride of place centered in front of the bare bay windows in the dining room. Within, an assortment of old bottle-brush trees populates a snowy churchyard, and a few leftover trees stand sentry outside. On clear, bright days, the sunshine twinkles brilliantly on the greenhouse panes.

ON A SIMPLE TABLE, A CHRISTMAS TABLEAU

An old kitchen table becomes the stage for a gathering of disparate pieces. Under a loopy conifer valance, a collection of family photos keeps company with a papier-mâché rabbit, a vintage wood finial, and a miniature vanity, among other pieces. Under the table, a wonderful old cast-iron carousel horse still carouses, this time wearing a collar of pine and ribbon. Rabbit, horse, vanity, finial: What an unlikely combination, but all together they say Christmas.

*To dress your home
for this frosty holiday of joy,
collaborate with Nature.*

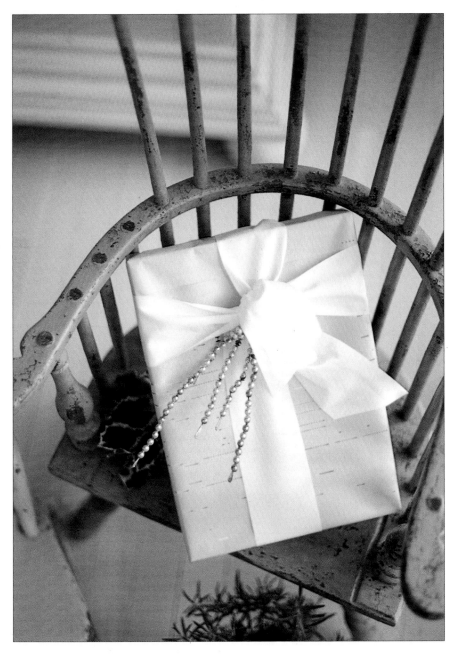

WINTER WHITE:
IT'S MORE THAN SNOW

In a sunroom such as this, the paler tones of decorations—rather than a traditional display of green and red—convey a feeling of Christmas serenity. With an eye to the different levels of the room, the homeowner has started at the top of the armoire, which holds a casual arrangement of pine boughs. Bouquets of variegated holly in pale sap buckets hang from white ribbon. And like so many fluffy clouds, pots of paperwhites and other white blossoms are set about the room. Where to hang the wreath with its miniature watering can? Why, on the garden trellis, of course.

WRAPPING IS A THING OF
BEAUTY, NOT SKILL

The wrapping of a present—every present, really—is as much a part of the holiday experience as the gift itself. If you think you're all thumbs when it comes to making bows, try something else. Gather wide satin ribbon into a simple knot and tuck several stems of glass beads inside. Wander about the entire house in search of other quirky decorations: gloriously gaudy costume jewelry from the 1950s, fancy chopsticks, silk flowers, sprigs of ivy, silly little dolls, wax fruit, or even old toy cars—whatever suits your fancy.

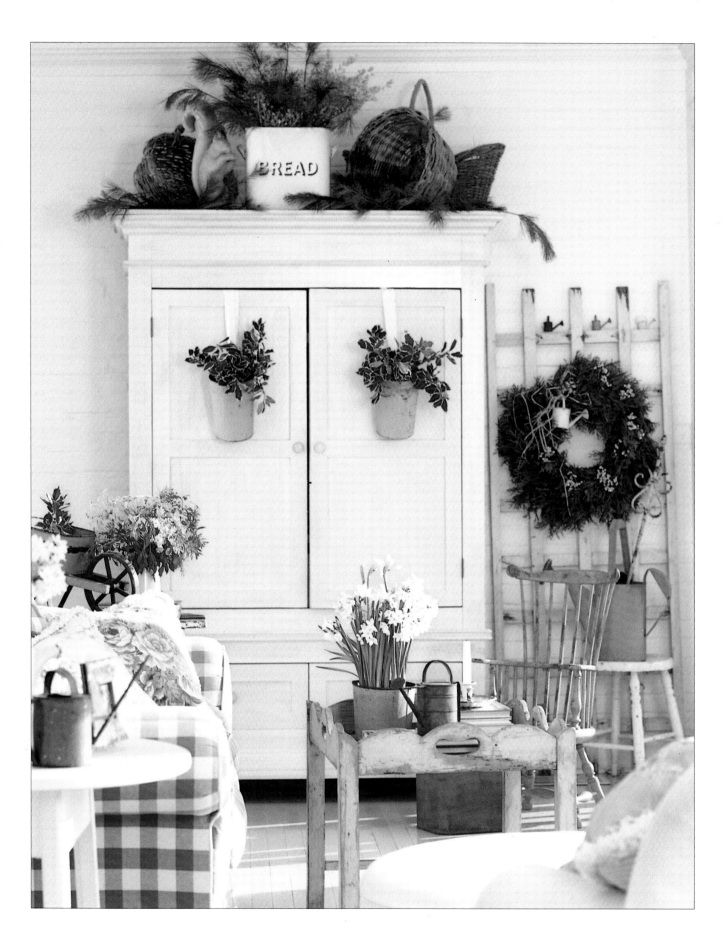

Giving

AS THE QUEEN OF EVERYTHING, I present here my etiquette of giving. Give what you know will have special meaning to the recipient. Give the most *in*expensive item if you know it will make someone's heart sing a bit. I would never give a friend an empty picture frame: I would slip in a photograph of her, the two of us, the place where she honeymooned, or her favorite breed of dog (you'll never go wrong with a Scottie—and they do photograph so well).

I adore giving presents to my husband, Phil. I've said that if my family had to live on my cooking, we'd all starve in a really cute kitchen. But Phil (maybe out of necessity) is a master cook. I am always on the lookout for something he'll enjoy; I pretty much have memorized what cooking equipment he has, I know all his cookbooks (no small accomplishment!), and I am even familiar with the contents of his utensils drawers—though I certainly don't want to learn how to use them. I get good clues by watching him cook; when he grumbles about a "darned hand mixer," I'll pick him up a new one. While flicking through cooking magazines, he'll see a new bread he'd like to bake. So that Christmas I'll give him the equipment and ingredients—and I'll have a wonderful new culinary treat!

I want my friends to have special gifts, too. If a friend asks me where I got my fabulous scarf, I'll order one for her. It makes me laugh when we turn up somewhere in the same stylish accessory. I love to give friends something they've admired in the past, perhaps a bracelet or a pillow I bought one day when we were flea-marketing together.

When you give something you love, you don't really give it up; you pass it on. Giving isn't competition, or about "spending the right amount," if spending is measured in money, that is. It is only about spending the right amount of thoughtfulness, caring, and spirit. If you think about what you cherish, it's probably not perfume or jewelry, but a frame with a photograph of someone you love, smiling into the camera.

Mary

CHRISTMAS COUNTDOWN
TURNS WAITING INTO FUN

Advent mittens—a clever alternative to the traditional paper calendars—make counting the days a treat.

✂ MAKE IT YOURSELF **PAGE 118**

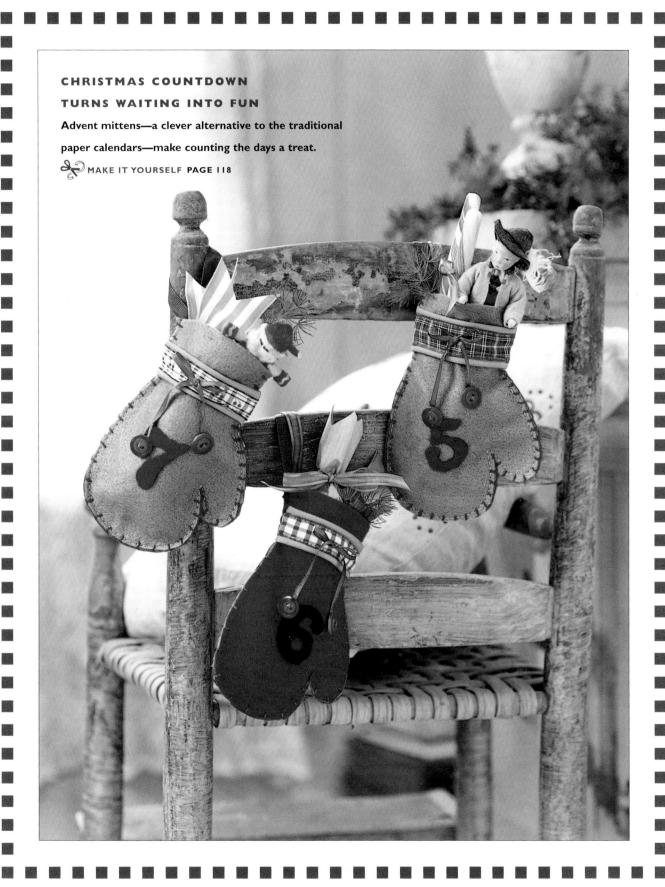

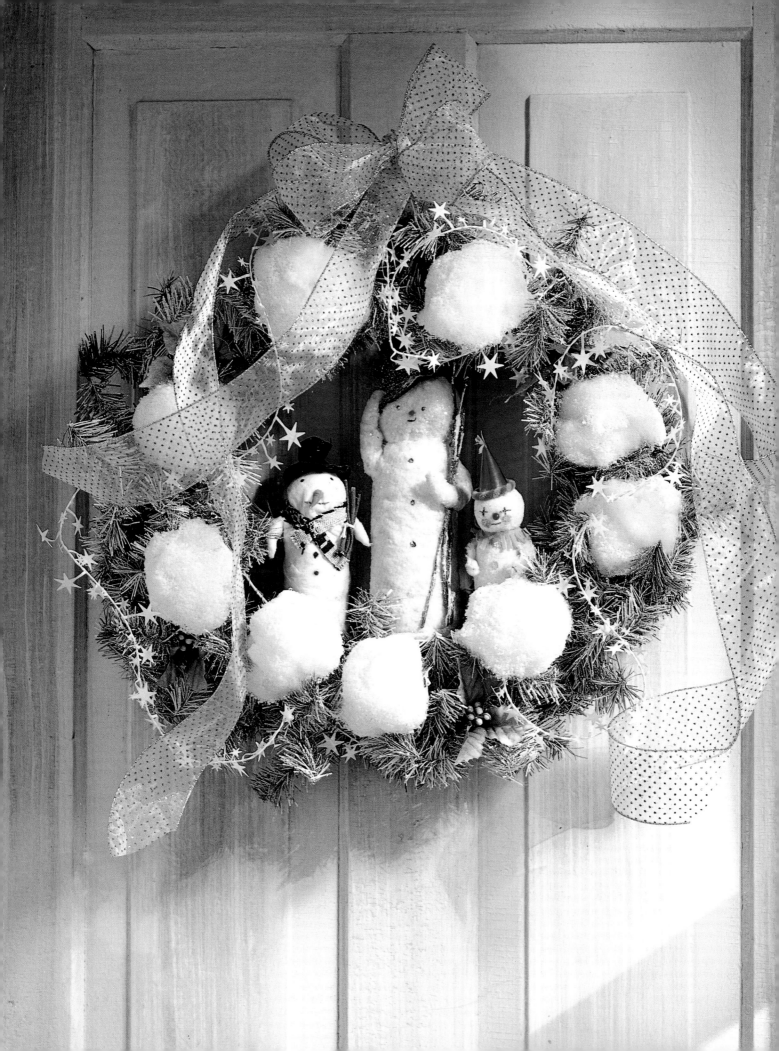

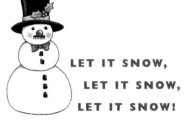

LET IT SNOW, LET IT SNOW, LET IT SNOW!

Snow is the icing on the Christmas cake. It's clean and new and fantasy-like. Snow won't keep in the house, but we can pretend. How better than a heavenly snowball wreath, complete with snow people (there's a clown in every family), foil stars, and yards of dreamy sheer ribbon. This wreath looks as lovely on a mirror or surrounded by a large empty picture frame as it does on a door.

✂ MAKE IT YOURSELF **PAGE 119**

SNOW BUSINESS

The English have their Christmas crackers, and we have our snowballs. Our snowballs? Yes, indeed, plump, lumpy snowballs of crepe paper, coiled round and round Styrofoam balls: As you wind the crepe paper around the balls, tuck charms and favors inside—tiny hearts, rings, miniature horses, lockets, silver bells and cockle shells, sour balls and red-hots. To finish the snowballs, dab some glue—any kind—at the end of the paper to keep it in place. Wrap the balls with wide gauzy ribbon and tie a name tag on each one or have a snowball grab bag.

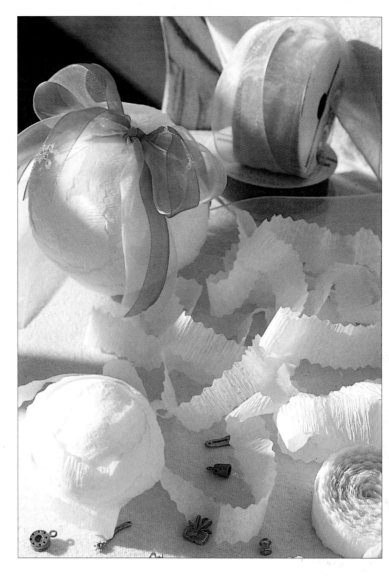

Create holiday decorations as free as a breeze or as packed as a snowball.

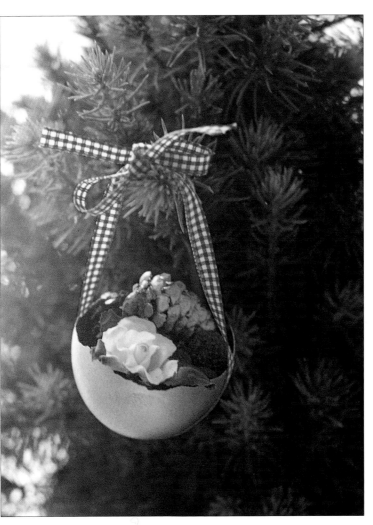

GOLDEN EGG CRADLES

Ukranians make intricately painted ornaments from eggs. Priceless Fabergé eggs are richly encrusted with jewels. But the ornaments here are from the shells of your breakfast omelet. Once they're rinsed and lightly sprayed with gold paint, they're wrapped in ribbon and filled with whimsical assortments of little charms: cranberries, rosebuds, tiny pinecones, buttons—whatever you like. An egg cradle kit makes a good gift for family or friends: Spray the eggshells, then pack them back in cartons and tuck in the fillings; tie it all together with some rich red rickrack or gingham ribbon and you'll be giving folks a good time.

✁ MAKE IT YOURSELF **PAGE 120**

A TOKEN TASSEL

It's Christmas dinner. You fuss over the food and table setting. Why not give diners a swingy favor like this spritely tassel, dangling invitingly over the back of each chair. Let your imagination run rampant; the ribbons (save those little bits too small for packages) and streamers can be swanky satin and silks or chirpy ginghams and checks. Finish the streamers with satin flowers, sourballs, or cherries. Make them all the same; make each one different—it only adds to the fun. Creating tassels also has a certain therapeutic value. Unwind from a day of shopping by plopping down with a sack of ribbon remnants and just loop away.

✁ MAKE IT YOURSELF **PAGE 121**

Why should Christmas cost a fortune? Mary has sweet ideas that won't break the bank.

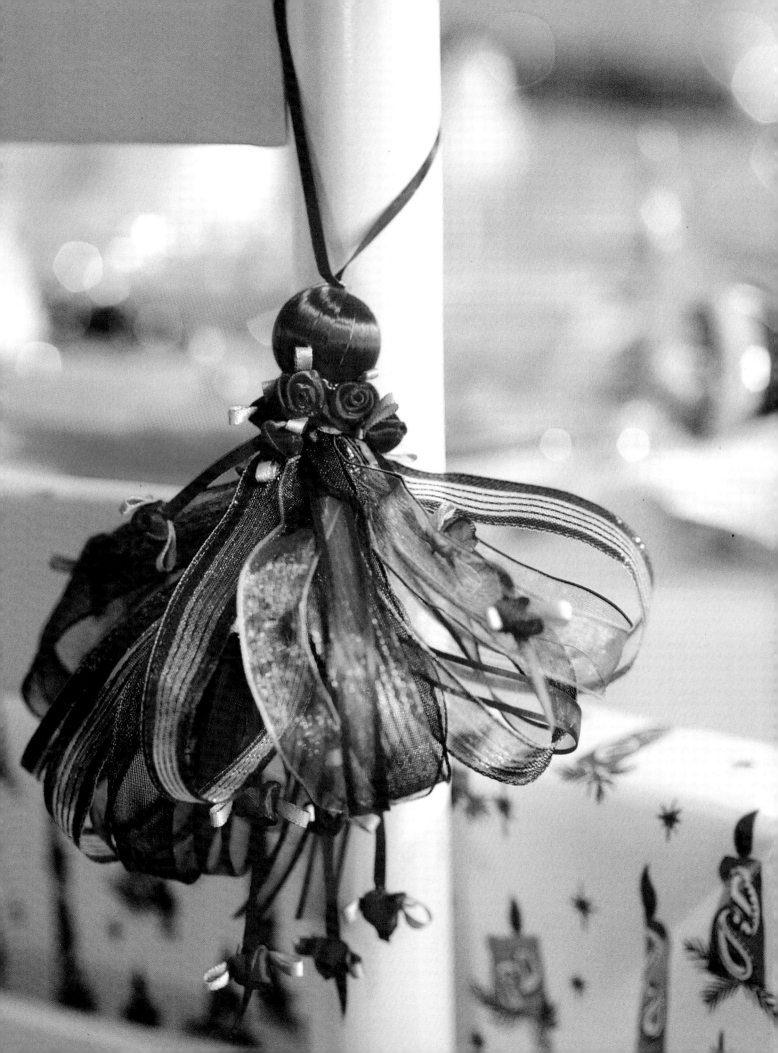

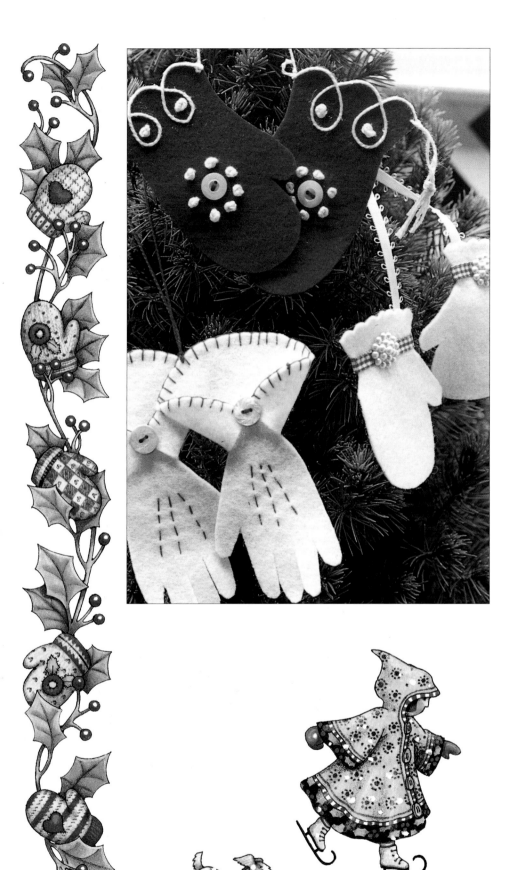

GLAMOROUS CHIC FOR THE WELL-DRESSED TREE

Felt is a wondrous fabric. It is remarkably versatile and easy to work with, and at Christmas it really comes into its own. Felt is synonymous with a handmade holiday, and one of our favorite ways to use it is in decorations for the tree. These darling gloves and mittens are the ones we like best. It's so satisfying to embellish them with buttons and beads you adore.

✂ MAKE IT YOURSELF **PAGE 122**

GOOD STUFF COMES IN SMALL PACKAGES

Pine needle pillow sachets look and smell like Christmas in the Rocky Mountains. These little gestures—about the size of postcards—are decorations that can be gifts, too. Cut from linen, they're decorated with holiday rubber stamps and blanket-stitched closed. The red and white of this trio have all the snap of peppermint candy canes. If you prefer, you can fill them with dried lavender or rose petals; but for a lingering scent of Christmas, do choose pine needles. In place of the rubber stamps, you could embroider a name or the year. Leave sachets on pillows for overnight guests, or tuck them into a gift basket of presents, or send them out as Christmas cards. They'll freshen the linen shelf, coat closet, a wool cap, even a pair of boots.

✂ MAKE IT YOURSELF **PAGE 123**

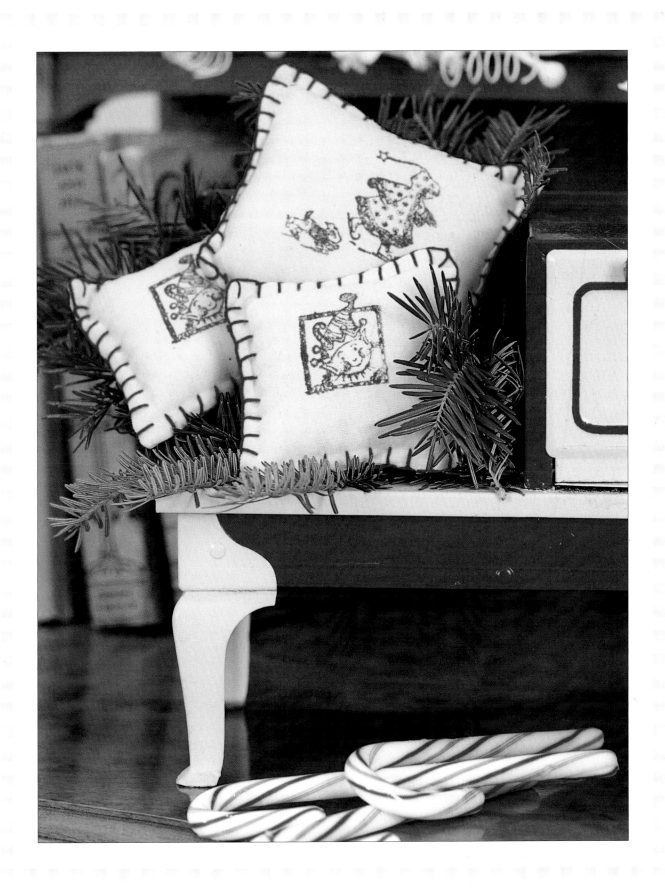

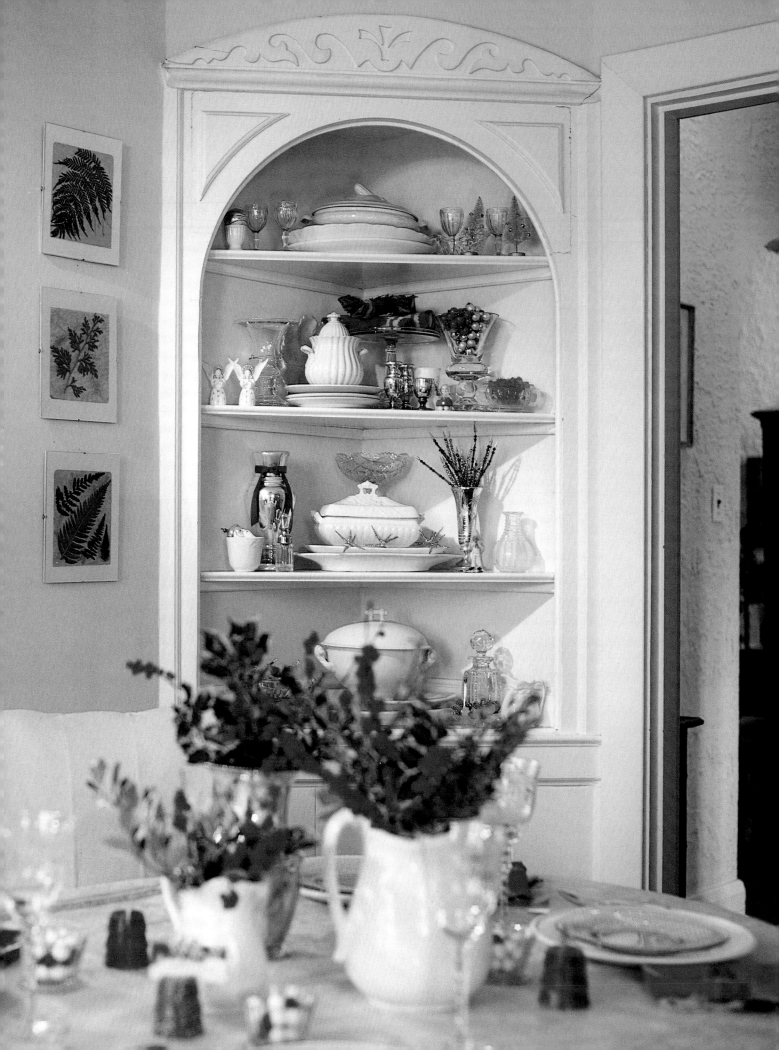

CHRISTMAS CUBBY

What's everyone's favorite room to decorate at Christmas? Probably the dining room. It makes sense, too, after all: The best serving ware is already displayed there, the lighting is flattering, and it's a safe area for fragile or treasured decorations. Tucking in holiday cheer brings it all to life. Each of the shelves in this cupboard features something remarkable, from the trees on top to the Christmas crackers below, and even the addition of the rich red velvet ribbon tied on a slender mercury glass vase.

REINDEER FAMILY

They're not the type to feast on your garden lettuces, so you can relax and welcome vintage celluloid reindeer indoors for the holiday. This unusual family could be tourists from the North Pole, poised on a snowy doily, with Dad guiding the way in his white ribbon collar. They look right at home with the silver tinsel trees and appear to be absolutely captivated with the holiday decorations throughout the room.

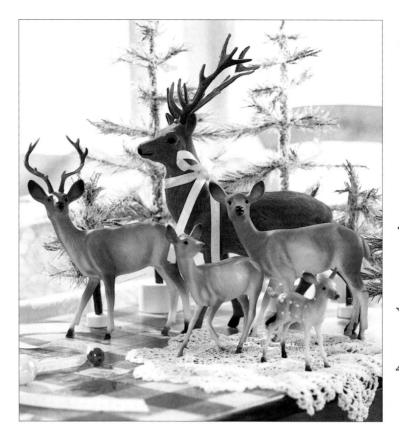

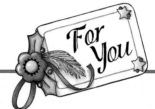

*Forget those last-minute phone calls before your big holiday party. Mail out **"save the date" cards** to remind folks well ahead of time. You'll have more guests and fewer missed—and embarrassed—friends!*

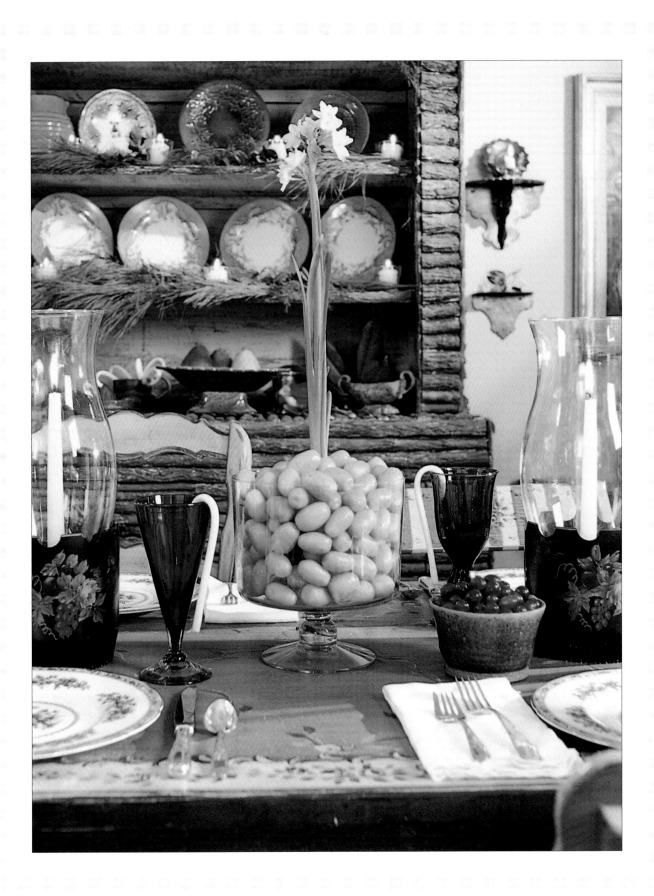

SPLENDOR IN THE KUMQUATS

Fresh flower centerpieces are so popular at Christmas, but let's face it—flowers are fragile and arrangements take a lot of time to create. Some homeowners, however, have figured out how to quickly put together intriguing, one-of-a-kind table art that will last, and that guests will admire for its cheeky charm. Here, a slender stalk of forced paperwhites reigns over dozens of kumquats (they hide the plant's little pot) in a pedestal trifle bowl.

EARRINGS FOR YOUR ORCHIDS

Yes, please, do dress your houseplants for the holidays. What could be more flirtatious than an exquisite orchid bejeweled with featherweight ornaments? Four tiny glass beads have been attached to the plant's stem with ordinary copper wire. To create the little curlicues, twirl the wire around a pencil or knitting needle, depending on how delicate you want them to look. Because everything is so light, there is no danger the stem will be perilously weighted down.

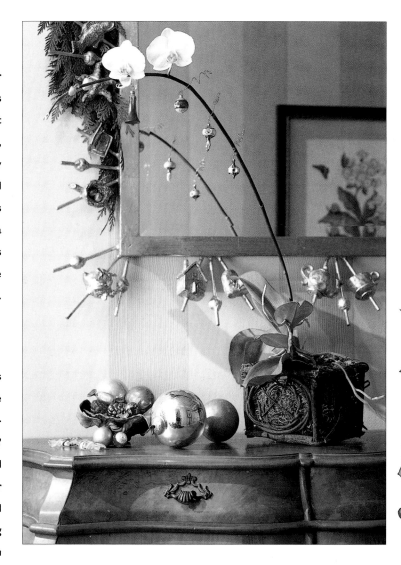

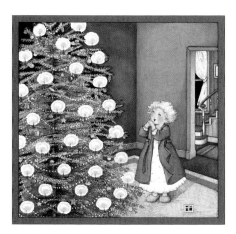

*Go ahead—
it's Christmas—
decorate every little thing
in the house.*

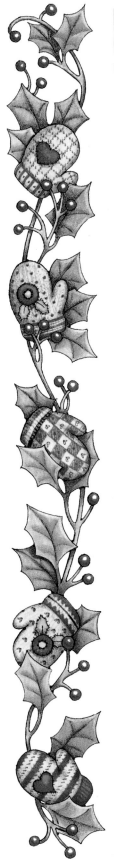

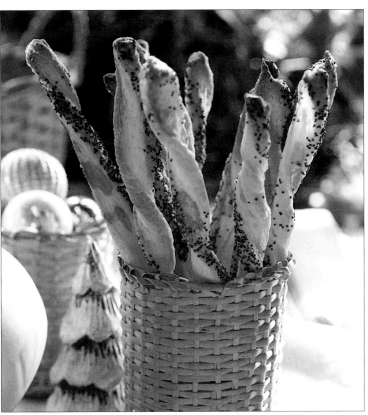

CHEESE STRAW, ANYONE?

Break out the puff pastry! Exceptionally fine puff pastry—the kind made with pure butter—is available at most good food shops and it's really just as delicious as the homemade version. Flavor some straws with sesame seeds and garlic, some with poppy seeds and blue cheese. Cheese straws make terrific presents, too, for hostesses, carolers, and un-expected guests, and for saying thank you to your mail carrier. Wrap up the straws in heavy cellophane and tie your packages with raffia or cotton string.

MAKE IT YOURSELF **PAGES 95 & 96**

IT'S THE NUTTIEST TIME OF THE YEAR

Fit for your favorite company, flavored nuts balance out every cocktail, from a glass of sherry to a bottle of beer. Our assortment features herb-crusted pecans and spicy honey almonds, both slow roasted to golden goodness. When you get them ready for the table, set the scene with a 1950s cotton Christmas tablecloth. Then surround the bowls with snowy miniature trees, pinecones, and a couple of woodland creatures. Put out several small bowls of each nut, and there you have it—a nut lover's idea of heaven.

MAKE IT YOURSELF **PAGES 97 & 98**

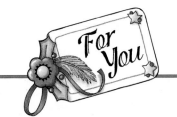

*Heat up a kettle of hot **mulled wine or cider**, and relax in front of the fire. If you have any left over, you can refrigerate the mixture for several days, then reheat it to fill the house with a tangy fragrance.*

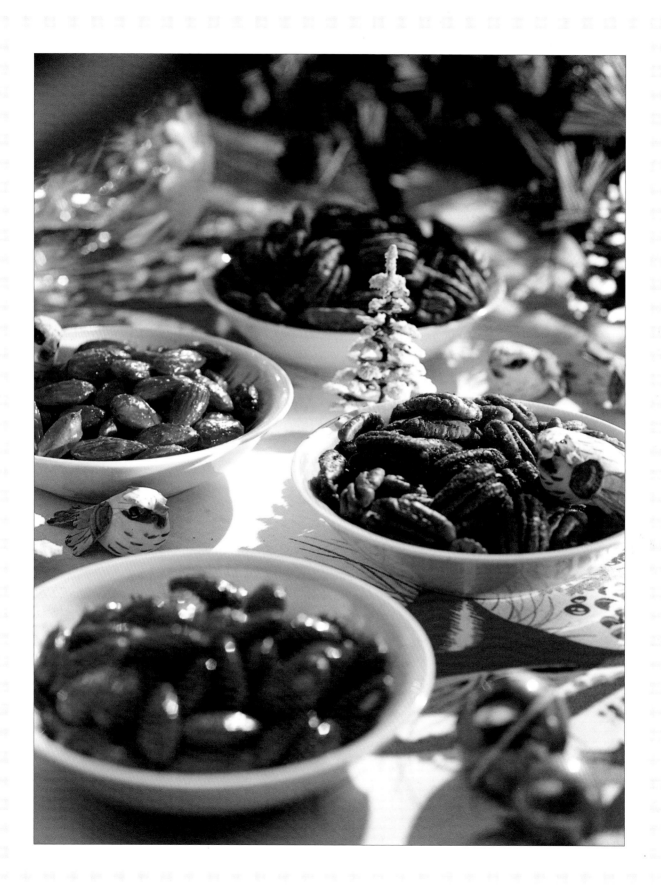

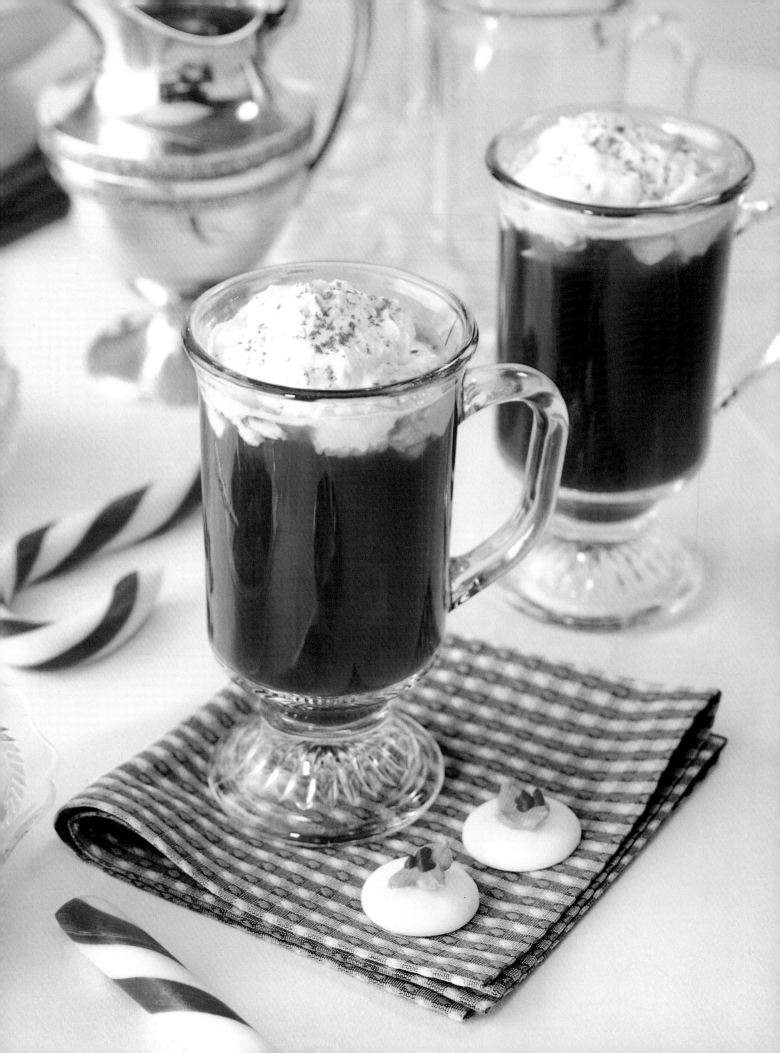

COFFEE WORTHY OF CHRISTMAS

This is a guaranteed chill-chaser. Brew up some coffee—make it strong—and offer it to guests with a choice of liqueurs: Drambuie for sweet tooths, Godiva for chocolate lovers, and crème de menthe for those who just can't get enough green at Christmas. Plop a dollop of whipped cream in each cup, and sprinkle grated chocolate over the cream. Set out candy canes instead of spoons to stir things up.

SWEET SEDUCTION

Lucky is the person who is about to try truffles for the first time—serious chocolate lovers must feel envy that the lucky soul is so near such bliss. Heavenly mixtures of chocolate, cream, and (as if that's not enough) sometimes butter, truffles epitomize holiday extravagance.

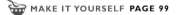 MAKE IT YOURSELF **PAGE 99**

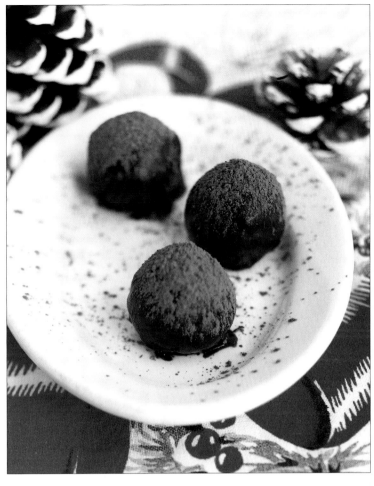

Christmas evenings are warmed with spirited coffee and French truffles.

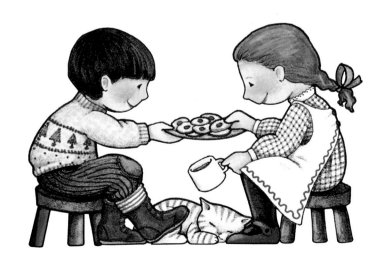

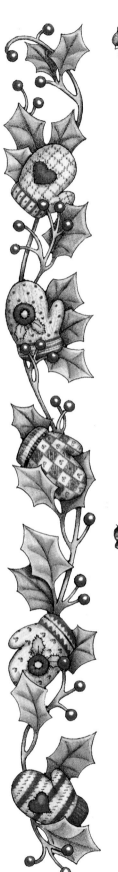

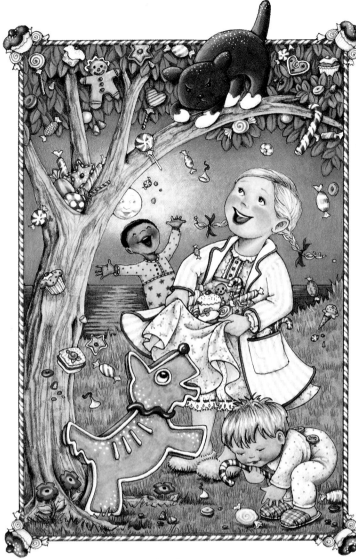

THE TEN
ALL-TIME BEST
SUGARPLUMS

Gingerbread boys & girls

Candy canes

Sugar cookies

Shortbread petticoat tails

English trifle

Peppermint drops

Chocolate truffles

Pecan tartlets

Bûche de Noël

A Bowl of Cherries

Here is the dessert called The Quintessence of Joy, Rapture of the Palate.

BONNIE BÛCHE DE NOËL

Making the French Christmas cake, Bûche de Noël, is work, no doubt about it. But once it's on the table, you'll know every minute was worth it. The famous dessert that's shaped like a forest log is actually tender chocolate cake sprinkled with kirsch and covered with whipped cream, then rolled into its distinctive log shape. The "logs" are slathered with dreamy ganache and then garnished with chocolate bark. For those who like to eat something healthful at every meal, strawberries are just the ticket. It's hard to imagine Bûche de Noël served any time other than Christmas, and it's hard to imagine one everyone wouldn't adore.

MAKE IT YOURSELF **PAGE 100**

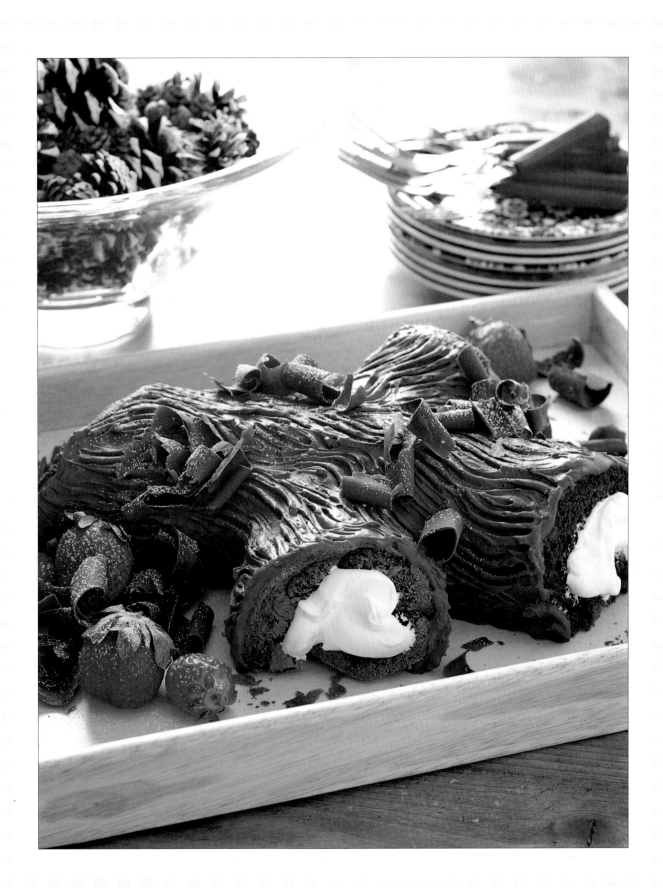

LET THE MERRYMAKING BEGIN

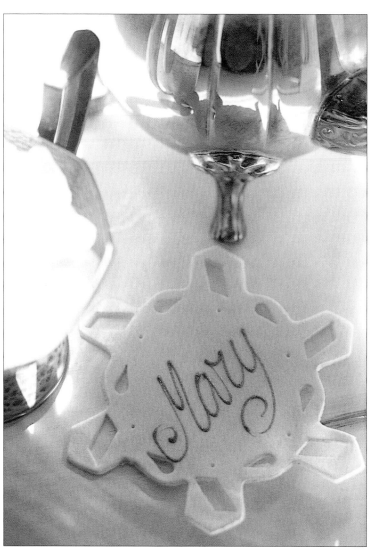

PLEASE BE SEATED

This is the prettiest place card you're ever likely to see, and it can be taken home to become a tree ornament or a keepsake. Designed by a talented baker in New York City, it's made of rolled fondant (the covering you often see on formal wedding cakes), then trimmed with a cutter or freehand with a knife into any number of snowflake designs. Add the names with piping gel in a pale color; you may have to practice "writing" on a flat plate first.

MAKE IT YOURSELF **PAGE 124**

PARTY FOR A STARRY, STARRY NIGHT

Twigs make the tree, vintage ornaments swing from ribbon holders, and sparkly stars dance about. Here is a dessert party that's pure fantasy. Set the table with a heavy white cloth—here a snowy quilt. Arrange cookies and pastries on a tiered stand. For party favors, create these adorable hankie purses: They're made with the delicate old linen handkerchiefs you see all year at flea markets and online auctions. Whatever their patterns, they all go together, so they needn't match.

Every visible thing in this world is put in the charge of an angel.

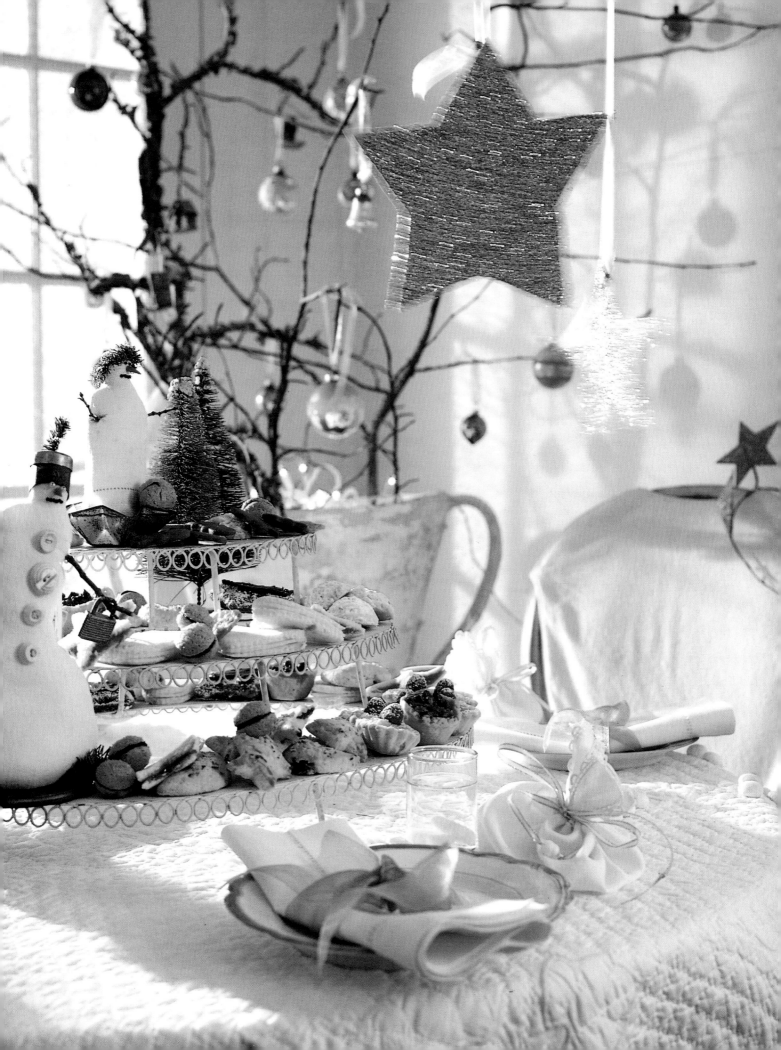

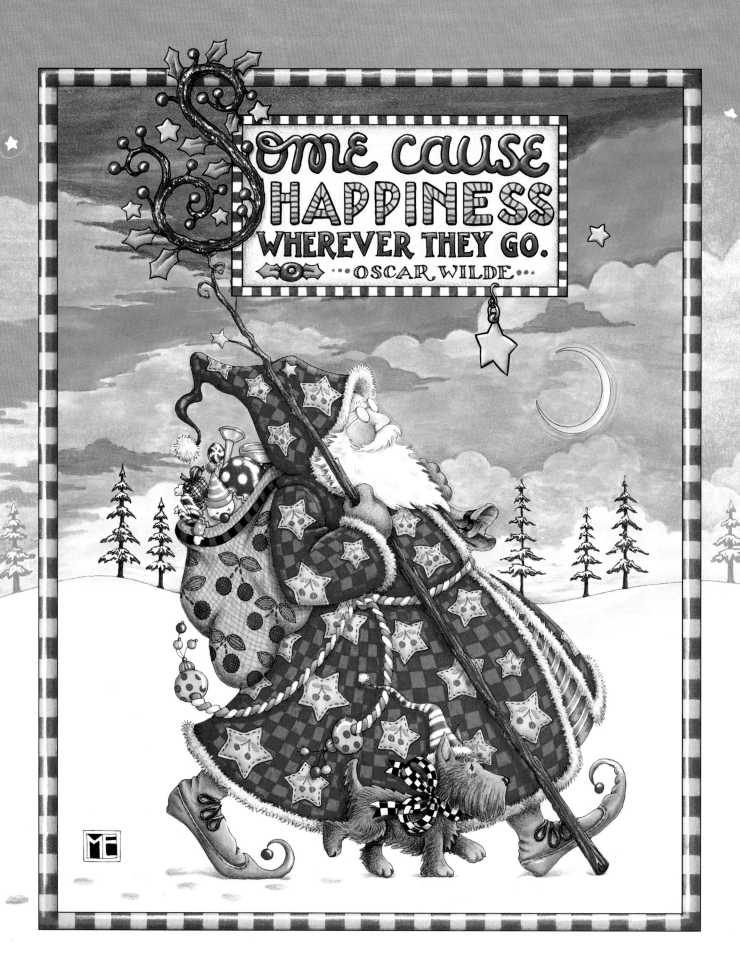

SCOTTIES & CHECKS

The mystery,
the magic,
and the
merriment—
this truly
is Christmas!

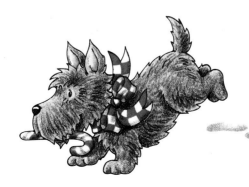

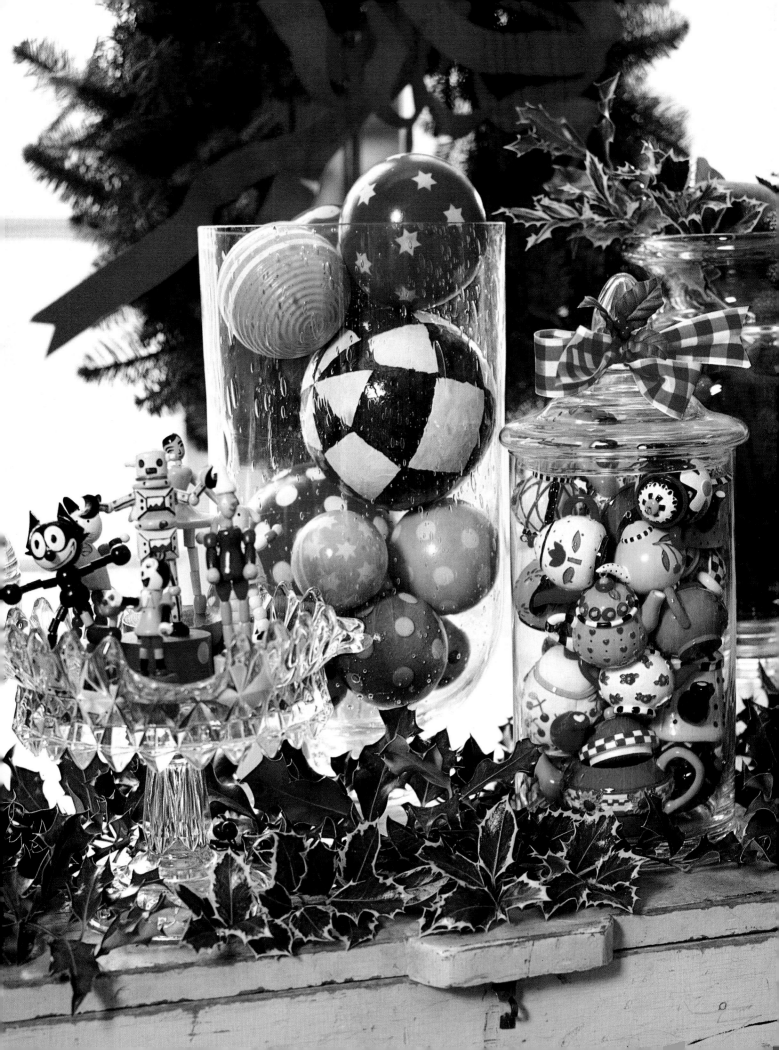

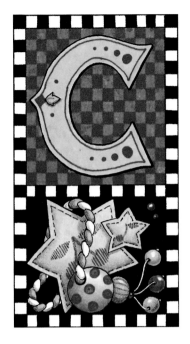

christmas always brings you back to childhood. The memories, some sentimental, some hilarious, are gifts you keep for yourself. There's the Lionel train set circling the tree, going around the villages and through the tunnels, toppling from the bridge on every other run. Remember the Schwinn bicycle with its handlebar streamers? And the dolls, the glorious dolls, just waiting to have their hair brushed and their toes counted? Give your family and guests the joy of toys. Christmas is about make-believe and the delights of youth. The real magic of Christmas is that you never outgrow it. Thank goodness you don't!

Mary's Christmas Means Time to Play

CHRISTMAS AT MARY'S is a fresh adventure every year. She's saved decorations since she was a young girl, and it's a whopping understatement to say that each year she adds more of everything to her collections. In fact, her attic could pass for a holiday warehouse, with dozens of cartons marked "Careful—Christmas Inside!"

A visitor will never see the same Mary Engelbreit Christmas a second time; each December, the holiday is reinvented. Years ago, Mary and an artist friend spent days constructing a papier-mâché castle. For his annual visit, Mary surprises him by setting up the castle somewhere unexpected.

At the Engelbreit home, wreaths of all types appear overnight: some of fresh greens with fat polka-dot bows and cherry ornaments; one of antique toys; one of felt scotties chasing one another in a circle; another of snowballs that never melt. And there are plenty of Christmas trees, too; after all, if one tree is a good idea, six are surely six times better.

Mary's enthusiasm for the holiday takes many forms besides her love of trees. If you

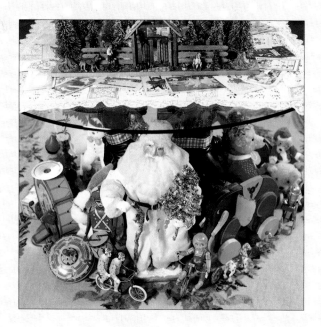

CHRISTMAS COMES HOME

The front doors open wide to welcome Christmas. Humble wooden houses with colorfully painted rooftops surround a small feather tree planted in a gift from the little drummer boy, almost as if it were the official village tree. The delicate branches hold dozens of playful toys and ornaments. Under a round glass-top table, Father Christmas presides over a battalion of tin toys and stuffed animals.

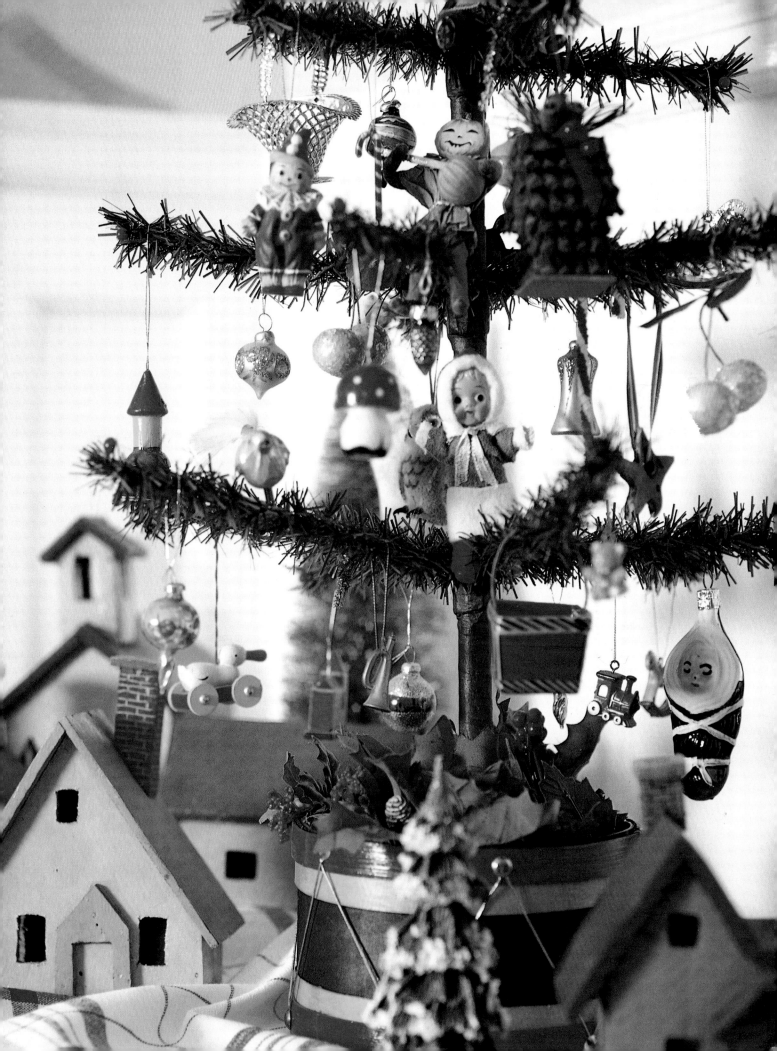

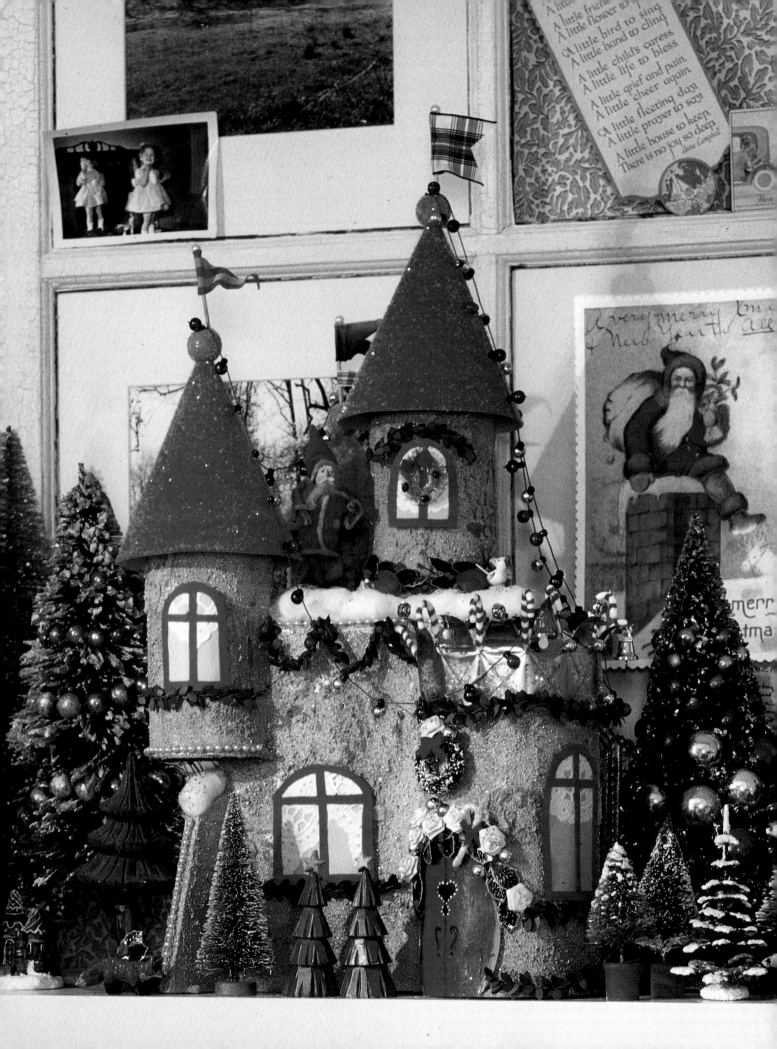

want to give your home the same kind of warmth, imagine what you can do. What do you collect? Your old teddy bears weren't made for Christmas, but they'd look so at home in a holiday display. If you're a basket collector, fill several with pinecones, toys, or glass ornaments. Pottery? It's perfect for bouquets of red roses, wands of glass beads, graceful bare branches. Grab colorful wood balls to stack up in a glass chimney or to dot the top of a lace-covered table.

The real secret to creating this Christmas wonderland is putting odd objects in unexpected places, all over the house. Tie a sprig of holly to a baseball with red kitchen twine; string the frames of artworks with twinkle lights; spray acorns with gold paint and pile them into a pair of Champagne flutes. Bring out the bride dolls and give them ribbons of tartan; put a jingle bell on your jack-in-the-box. And above all, always keep toys in your Christmas.

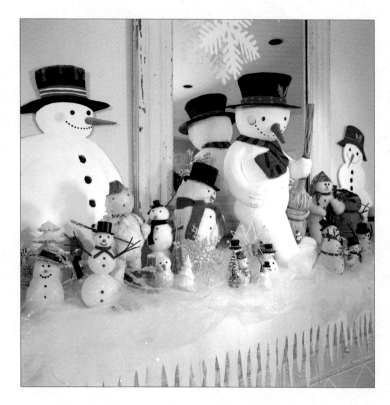

Let your decorations tell their stories: some poignant, some silly. Christmas is special for them, too.

CHRISTMAS IN A CASTLE

Want to have a castle you can enjoy year after year? Mary and a friend taped cardboard paper towel rolls and potato chip tubes together to form the turrets and curving corners. The whole castle was painted with acrylics and decorated with glass beads, peppermint sticks, little ribbon flags, and faux snow.

GENERATIONS OF THE SNOW FAMILY

On Mary's white mantel, her beloved snow folk swirl and twirl about on an ice pond made of gift-wrap tissue. They really don't match; though they all resemble each other in some way or another, each has its own whimsical charm. Together, the rag-tag bunch is delightful.

Wonder

I REALLY THINK CHRISTMAS made me want to become an artist. It certainly helped. I couldn't sketch fast enough to capture all the holiday wonder I saw. It was a feast tempting me to draw, to color, to create. There was plenty of visual stimulation—awesome decorations on neighbors' houses, shop windows filled with all kinds of gifts, Christmas tree stands surrounded by twinkling lights and starry night skies. I drew Santa and his elves over and over, and I drew the presents I wanted. I drew Christmas choirs and skating parties and angels in the snow. Each day I couldn't wait for the mail to arrive so that I could rip open those Christmas cards and be fascinated by their fantastic art. As I got older, I found so much more to be inspired by—the spirit of wonder that came along with the holiday.

I worked hard to get the feeling on paper, and when I look back now, so many years and so many drawings later, at that young girl's sense of Christmas, I feel all of those emotions again. Now I know that the wonder is real: We become the best we can be at Christmas, celebrating together the pleasures of life, the comfort of friends, the love of family.

Sometimes the wonder is right before us, in a tantalizingly wrapped present we can't wait to open, in the glory of the beautifully decorated tree. We hear it in a choir singing "Silent Night"; we applaud it at the Christmas pageant. We inhale it in the scents of fresh-cut greens, holiday meals, gingerbread baking, and a new snowfall.

We see it in the face of someone who has just opened the perfect gift. And we feel it in our own giving—to Toys for Tots programs, to pets living in animal shelters, to elderly friends in nursing homes, to someone spending the holiday in a hospital, to anyone in need of an unexpected act of generosity.

Have I lost my childhood sense of wonder? No, I don't think that's possible. I still believe in the magic of the season. But I believe in it even more now: I believe we pass the wonder on. Seeing the joy in the faces of children and the astonishment that goes with this magical season still brings me immeasurable joy. Now my Christmas artwork has the perspective of experience, but I am grateful that it has lost none of its innocence. For these few weeks at least, let wonder reign!

Mary

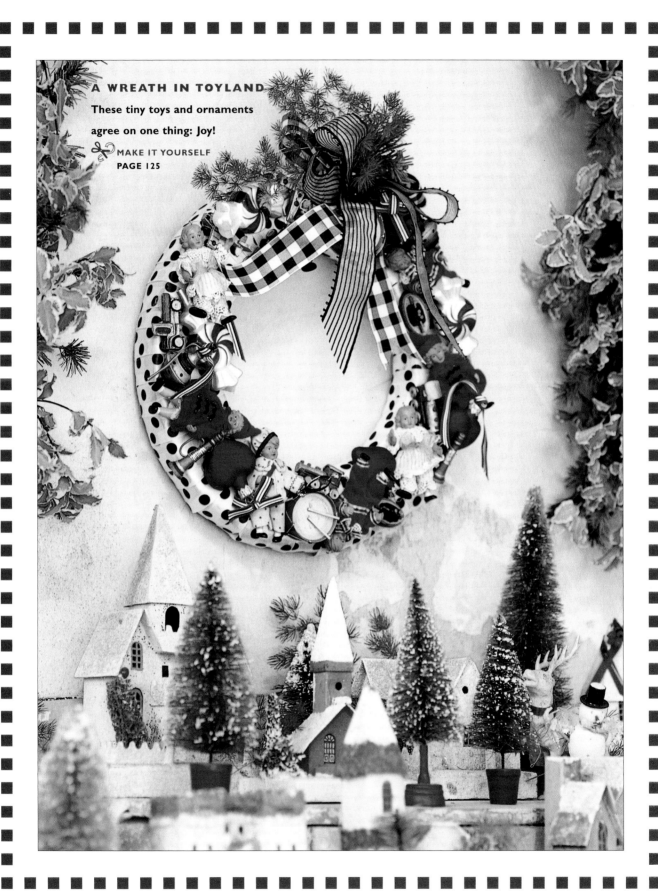

A WREATH IN TOYLAND

These tiny toys and ornaments
agree on one thing: Joy!

✂ MAKE IT YOURSELF
PAGE 125

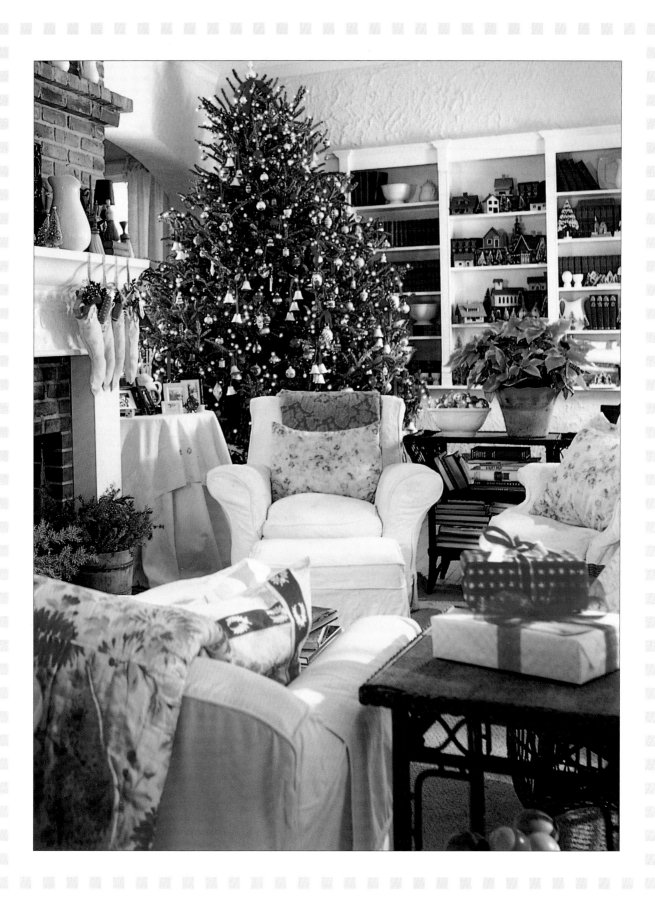

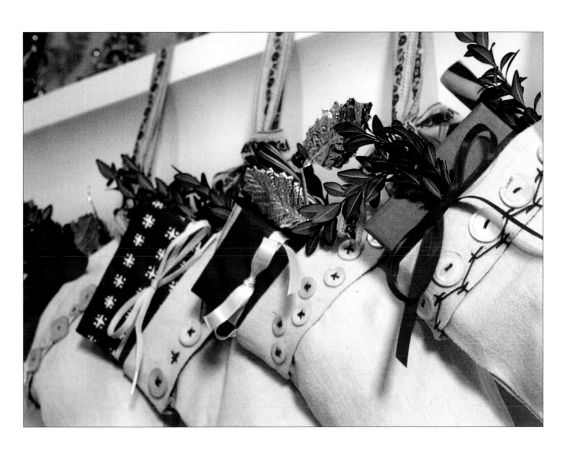

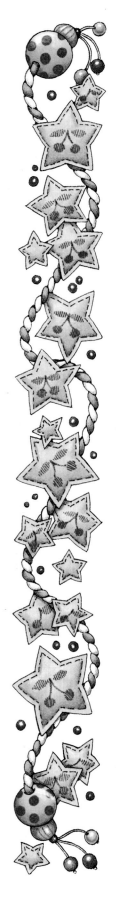

CANDY CANE CHRISTMAS

This entire decorating scheme for the holidays is a cheerful improvisation on the happy theme of red and white. The decorations are placed so well that the tree is impressive but not overwhelming. Antique glass ornaments and beads are set in silver trophy cups for a tabletop display; stockings are hung off-center on the mantel, leading the eye to the tree. The bookcases host collections of toy trees and houses from train sets. Wrapped packages are scattered about the room. The secret to this harmony? The red-and-white scheme is so versatile that even the simplest gestures, like red ribbons encircling white ironstone bowls and pitchers, send out a sweet note.

A room without stockings simply isn't dressed for the holiday.

VARIATIONS ON THE BUTTON THEME

Hung by the chimney with care, these tender stockings were made from linen table napkins—but damask tablecloths and kitchen towels and even old linen pillowcases will do. For yours, stitch simple designs with embroidery floss, and finish them with buttons sewn on using the same floss. Hang the stockings with ribbon as colorful as the details you've created, and your mantel will glow.

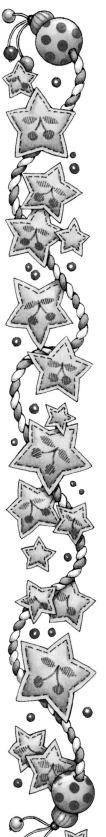

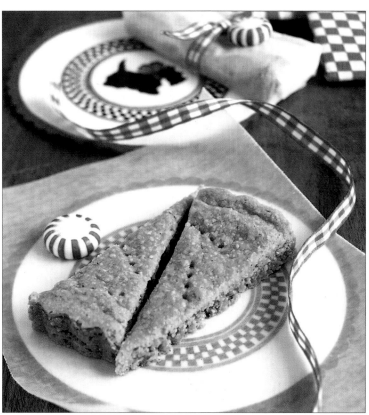

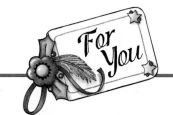

SHORTBREAD TAILS

Scottish shortbread is a longtime Christmas favorite. This has hazelnuts and oats for extra flavor; it's still made the traditional way, with lots of fresh butter, then cut into the famous wedge shapes called petticoat tails. Wrap the tails in wax paper tied closed with lengths of checked ribbon and give them to folks you see everyday—anyone who makes your day easier or a touch more special.

MAKE IT YOURSELF **PAGE 104**

WE LOVE ALL CHRISTMAS COOKIES, BUT MARY'S ARE THE BEST

If you believe that Christmas cookies deserve special treatment, you won't find any that say "Happy Holidays" better than Mary's Scotties and Toy Balls. Both are shaped with cookie cutters, and once they're baked the fun really begins. Piping the Scotties' shapes may take a couple of tries, but luckily there's no such thing as a homely Scottie. Brightly colored collars complement the red-and-white polka-dot balls, and you can just feel the playfulness between these two great friends.

MAKE IT YOURSELF **PAGE 102**

For You

Do you have a **homebound neighbor** whose family arrives en masse for Christmas? Drop by a day before to hang a **simple wreath** and some holiday lights. And don't forget the **cookies and milk**. Well-done!

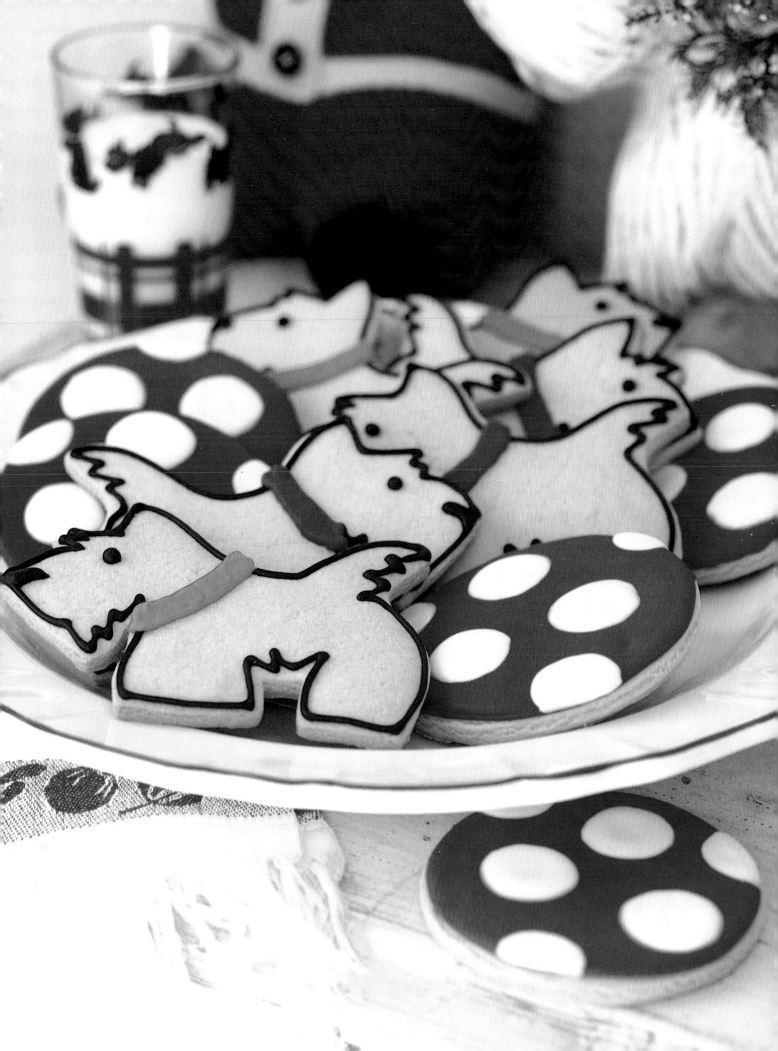

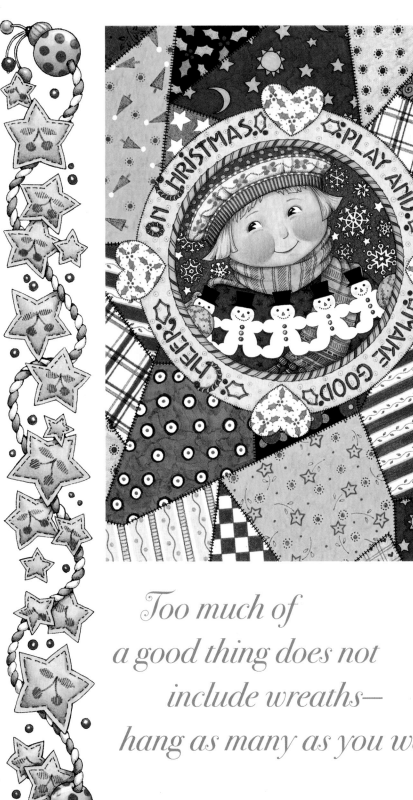

Too much of a good thing does not include wreaths— hang as many as you want!

EIGHT SCOTTIES CHASING

Have you ever thought of giving someone a wreath for Christmas? They are some of the best presents anyone can receive, because they can be featured in decorations almost anywhere in the house. This loveable one is made of fabric and ribbon so it can be brought out year after year. You can vary the colors of the pups, or make a wreath with all-white Scotties or all-tartan ones that will be admired in any room. Be sure to present your wreath in a sturdy box with lots of tissue so that it can be safely stored until next Christmas. It's a thoughtful gesture to tuck in several different ribbons, so the wreath can take on a new look each year. The sheer plaid looks wonderful in a bedroom; for the dining room, a wide ivy-on-cream ribbon or a red-and-white polka-dot pattern would make those playful Scotties even more energetic. A few sprigs of fresh pine can be tucked in among the puppies each December.

MAKE IT YOURSELF PAGE 126

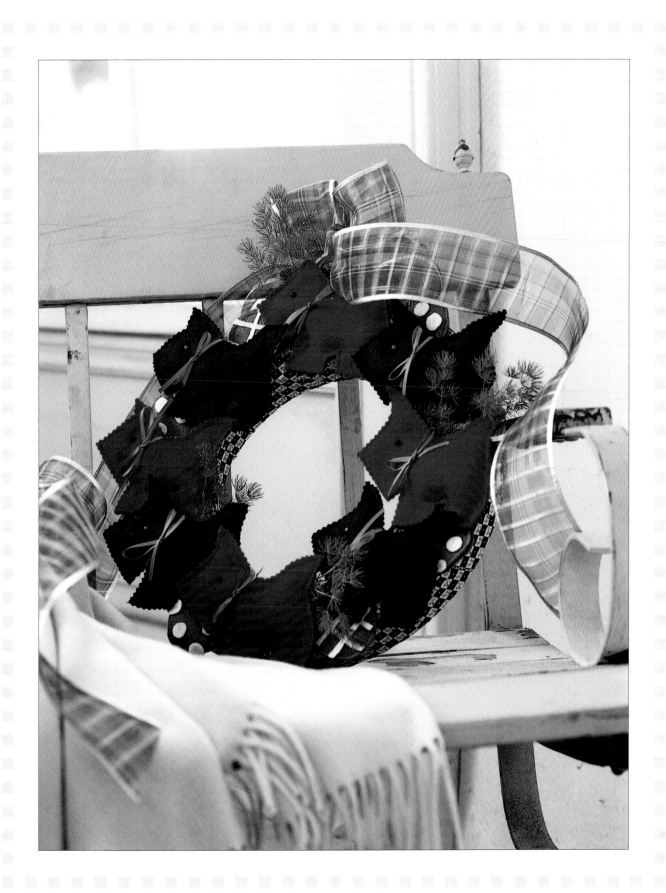

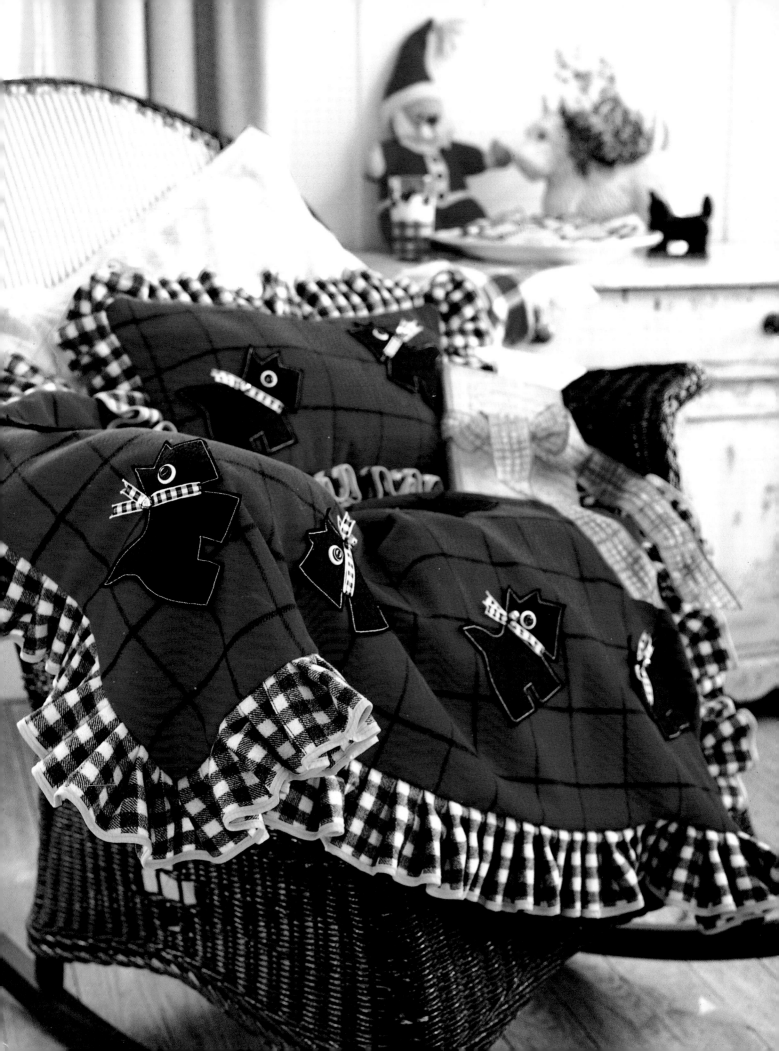

HOW ABOUT A CHRISTMAS SLEEPOVER?

Visitors are part of the pleasure of the holidays. Give youngsters who are staying with you, or perhaps just yawning for an afternoon nap, their own pillows and blankets. Who could resist sleep when they're all cozy and warm under a dozen Scotties? Dress the Scotties in snappy collars with jingle bells and button eyes; if you have babies or toddlers, you may want to wait until they're a bit older before sewing on the bells and buttons.

✄ MAKE IT YOURSELF **PAGE 127**

A SCOTTIE TO CUDDLE

A love for stuffed animals is something never outgrown, and thank goodness for that. This dapper fellow, complete with a red-and-white polka-dot sweater, is just waiting to be picked up and brought over to the sofa to keep you company as you read a good book or treat yourself to a short "dog" nap. He's just the right size for a car trip, too. He's an agreeable sort; just don't ask him to play fetch!

✄ MAKE IT YOURSELF **PAGE 128**

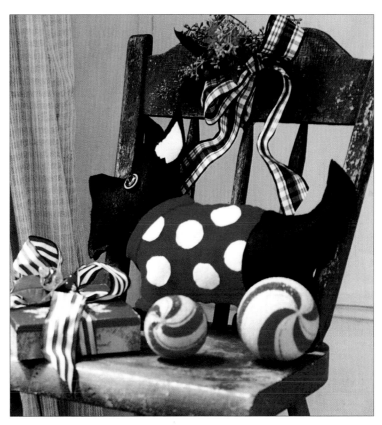

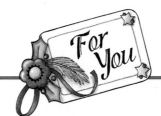

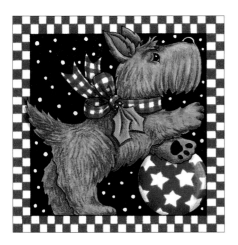

*Here's a **Christmas shortcut** from one of those super-organized women we all envy this time of year: Color-code **your to-do list**—green for decorating, blue for shopping and wrapping, and red for entertaining.*

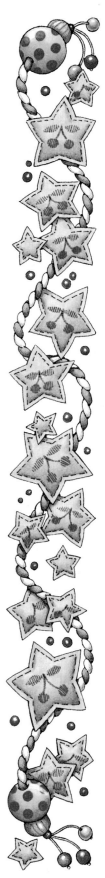

*Every room in the house
deserves at least one tree—
why else would there be
so many fabulous ornaments?*

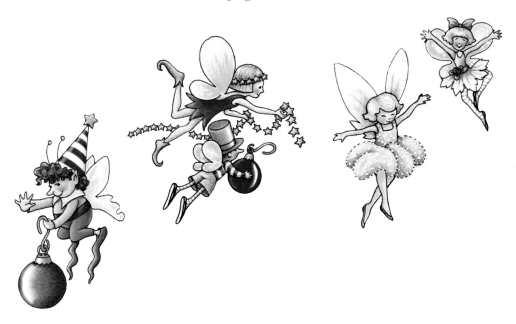

WITTY DRESS-UP FOR A HUMBLE LITTLE TREE

Imagine how wan this little tree was before Mary worked her magic on it. First, she "planted" it in a square terra-cotta pot and tucked in fresh greens. The branches are spaced so far apart that Mary knew they would perfectly show off her brand-new felt Scottie ornaments, which she hung with pretty check ribbon. Just for fun, she gave the pups a red felt ball to bounce after. Tiny glass ornaments are the jewels of the tree, and a fat candy-cane bow tops it all off. Keeping the tree company are a brightly wrapped present and a pair of Scottie bookends climbing up vintage books. The mantel hasn't been forgotten, but it also isn't overdone. A few bottle-brush trees, a Scottie menagerie, and a jumbo polka-dot ball congregate to watch over the tree. Behind the gold framed mirror, Mary has tucked in some of her vintage holiday cards. This is the kind of vignette that makes your rooms really look like Christmas—a careful selection of pieces that are different enough but still harmonize beautifully.

MAKE IT YOURSELF **PAGE 129**

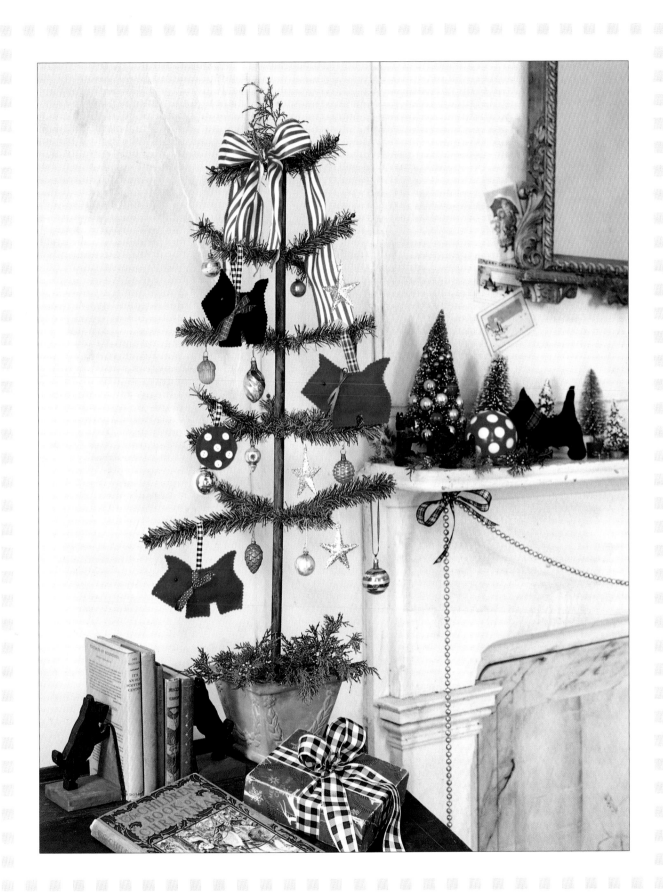

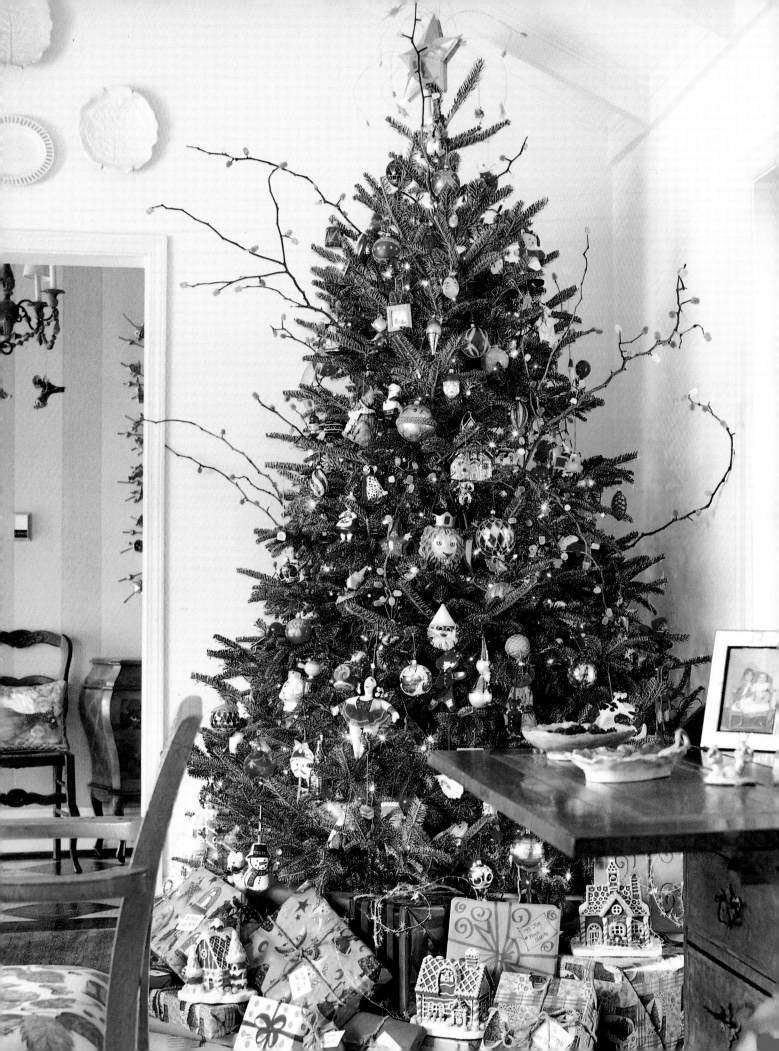

THE TEN ALL-TIME BEST CHRISTMAS PRESENTS

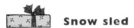

Rocking horse

Snow sled

Toy boat

Bride doll

Red wagon

Scooter

Ice skates

Baseball glove

Teddy bear

64-pack of crayons

ARTIST IN THE FOREST

Like snowflakes, no two Christmas trees are alike. Here is a Fraser fir with equal parts whimsy, wonder, and mystery. What's most unusual about this tree is its halo of branches: Graceful bare branches have been brought indoors, tipped with sugary gumdrops in neon-bright colors, and positioned so they seem to float out of the tree. Tiny twinkle lights flicker like stars in a winter's night sky. The tree's topper is a magnificent gold five-point star, itself surrounded by orbiting gold wires with tiny balls.

Beneath the tree are presents waiting to be packed and mailed to faraway friends. If you send gifts, you probably pack them with great care and once they've been mailed, begin to worry about crushed bows and missing name tags. Instead, try this: Wrap the boxes in heavy brown kraft paper or white butcher paper. Grab your felt markers or watercolors, and draw or paint those ribbons, bows, holiday greetings, name tags, or any kind of design right on the paper. You're a genius!

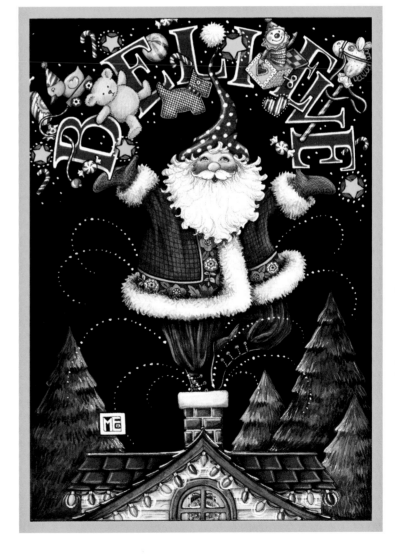

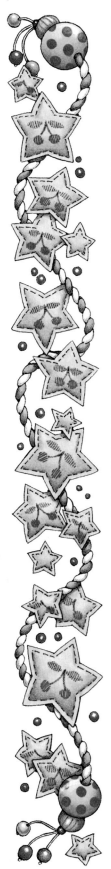

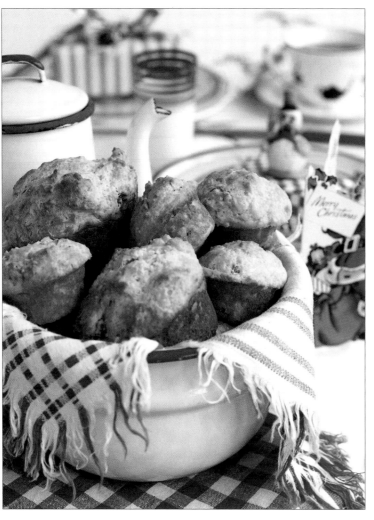

*Good morning—
welcome to the best breakfast
of the year!*

CHRISTMAS MORNING: LET'S ALL EAT!

You've finished Christmas Eve dinner and you've checked that Santa got all his presents under the tree. Now enjoy the morning. Forget fancy, fussy food; everybody will love prosciutto muffins with winter frittata. Of course, you'll want to make everything extra special, so try baking the muffins in two different pans, one with regular-size muffins and the other with tiny ones, for those who may already be filling up on sugarplums.

MAKE IT YOURSELF **PAGE 105**

A BREAKFAST TABLE OF WHOLESOME HOLIDAY FUN

Frittata, the wonderful Italian omelet that's baked in the oven, is quick, easy, and divinely delicious—and it even looks like Christmas. Our version is made with parmesan, mozzarella, red and green bell peppers (how much more Christmas could it be?) and garnished with fresh chives. Because frittata is good served warm, at room temperature, and even cold, it will wait until the gifts have been opened. Set the table with some vintage cards, a few toy roadsters, and perhaps a robot or two. Finish with a pitcher of orange juice and a pot of fresh coffee, and Christmas Day can really begin.

MAKE IT YOURSELF **PAGE 106**

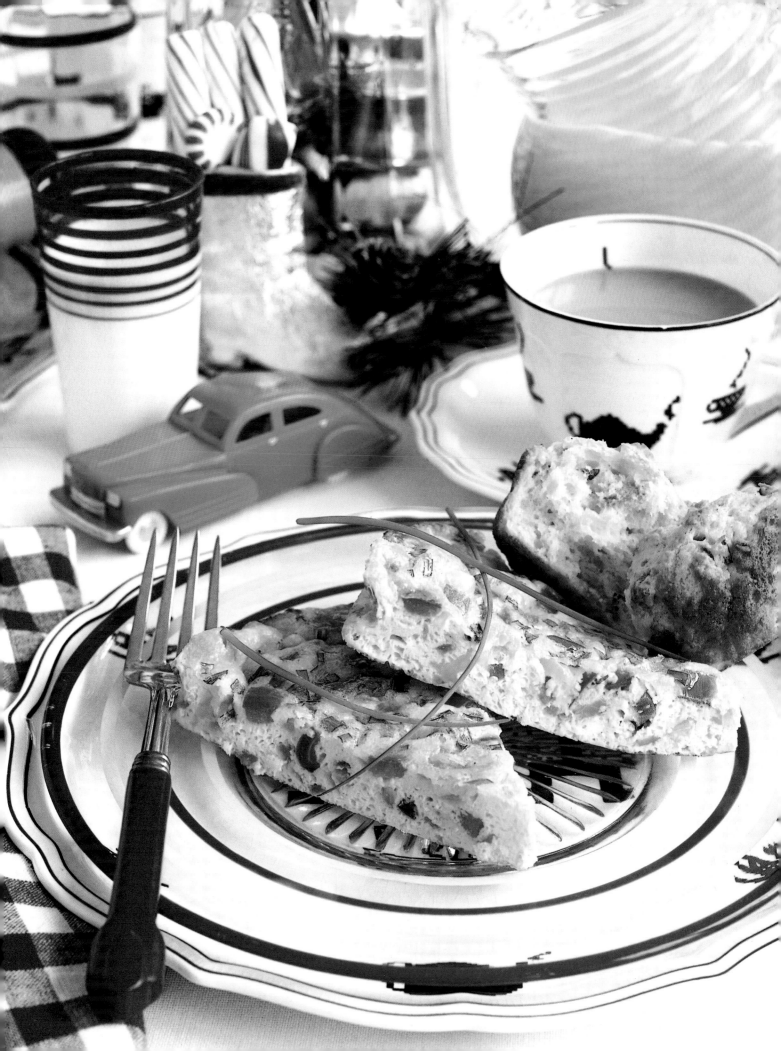

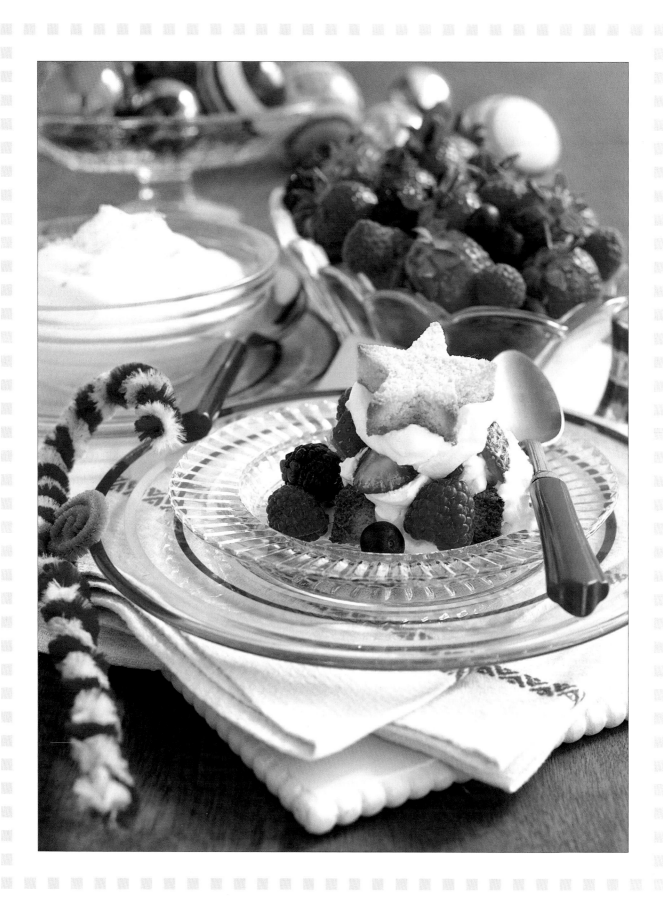

SWEET SURPRISE

Here is a marvelous dessert. Why is it so special, you ask? It's simple to make, it's mostly prepared well ahead of time, it's luxurious, it's got whipped cream, and it's full of fabulous, out-of-season fresh berries. This version has a heavenly maple poundcake and lemon-scented whipped cream, but you can make yours with purchased cake and ordinary whipped cream if you're short on time. But do slice the cake, cut the slices into stars with cookie cutters, and lightly toast the cutouts. Spoon on the cream and berries, and everyone will be charmed.

MAKE IT YOURSELF **PAGE 107**

CAUTION: BEARS AT PLAY

Do you have a collection of favorite old toys? Invite them to join in the celebration. Some of Mary's bears get bored just sitting around through all the Christmas festivities, so Mary sets them up with a game of dominoes. If the teddies are a little slow in getting into the spirit of the game, a passerby can surreptitiously make a play. Perhaps the next visitor will make another move—and maybe a whole game will be finished without a teddy ever lifting a paw.

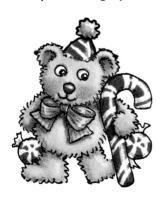

Here's the grand finale: Just when you thought the meal was over, you get to eat dessert—for breakfast!

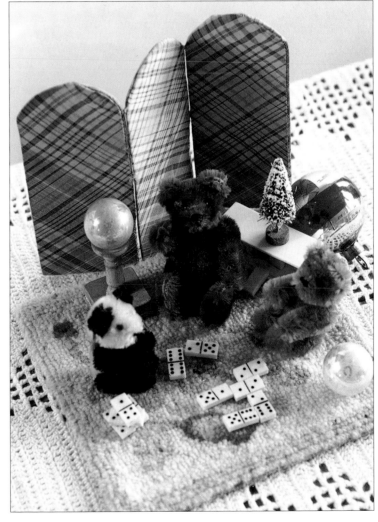

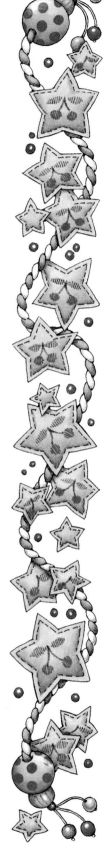

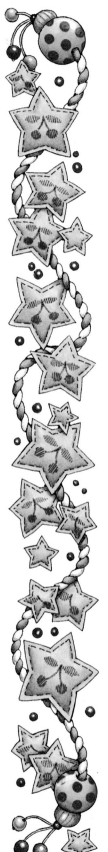

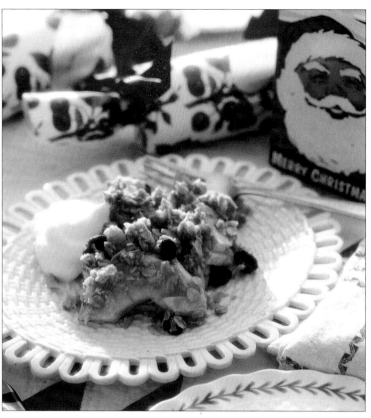

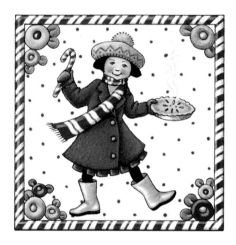

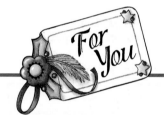

Setting the table *for the holidays doesn't have to be a chore. Gather a box of toys,* **Christmas crackers, vintage Santas,** *and snow globes. Vary them from meal to meal. Watch diners have fun as they savor good food and good talk.*

A WARM WELCOME

Everyone gets company during the holidays, whether it's family coming for the annual party or good friends who drop by unannounced. You needn't run to the refrigerator for the usual selection of cheese and crackers if you keep one or two desserts on hand. A couple of the very best are made with apples: Apple-Oat Crisp and heavenly French Apple Tart. Both will please any kind of palate and keep beautifully for a few days after baking. Dress them up with a snowfall of confectioners' sugar or a dollop of whipped cream. These desserts are also resilient travelers; when it's your turn to bring the sweet, you'll have no trouble arriving with either one in perfect shape.

MAKE IT YOURSELF **PAGES 108 & 109**

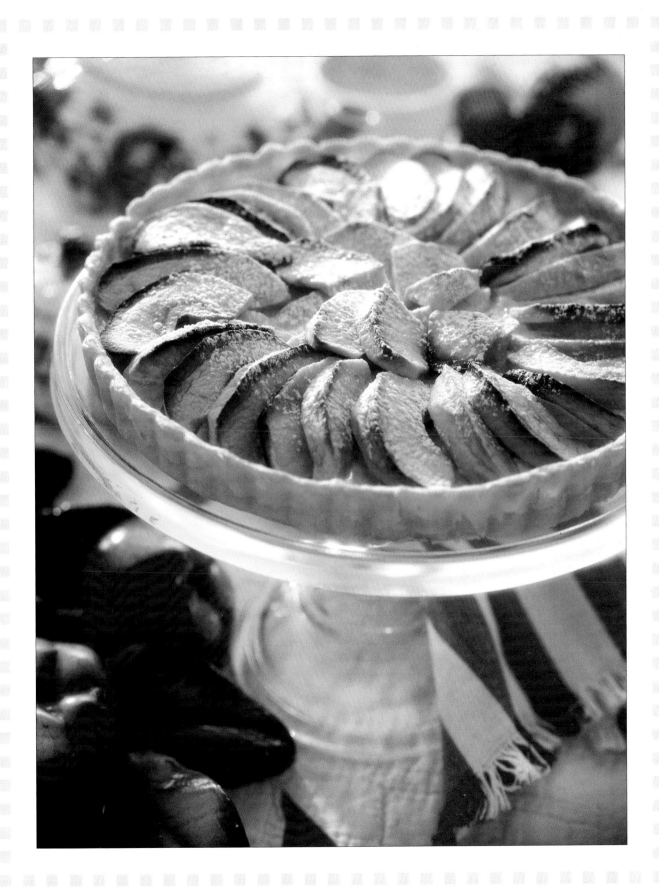

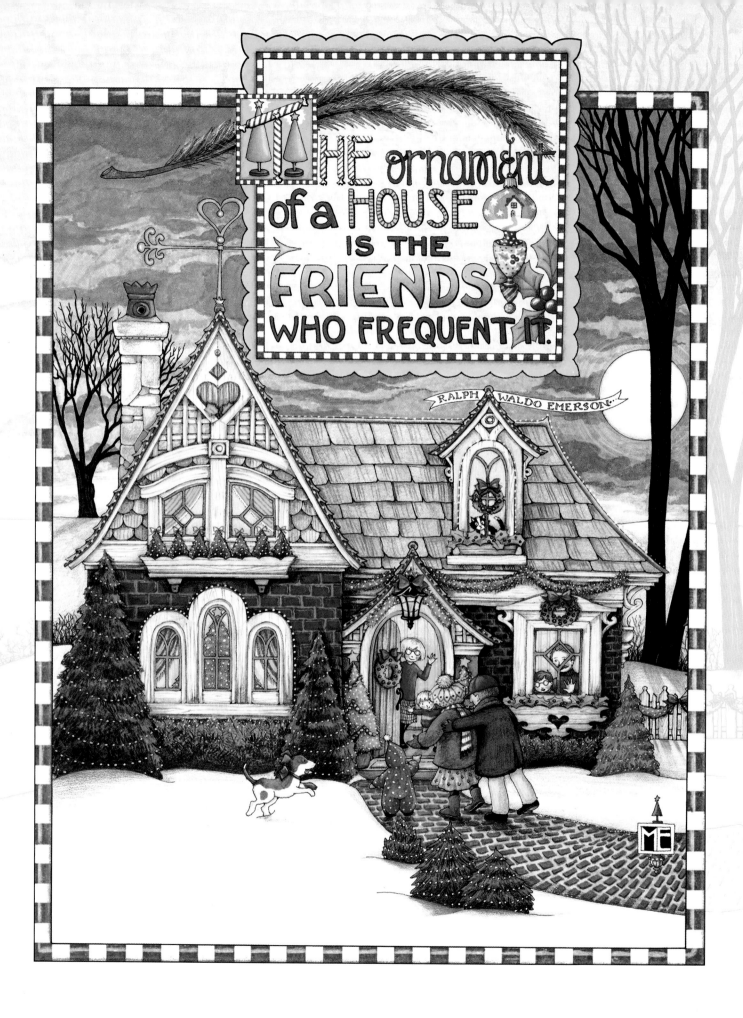

THE ornament of a HOUSE IS THE FRIENDS WHO FREQUENT IT.

RALPH WALDO EMERSON

COMFORT & JOY

We gather
together to
share again the
miracle of
Christmas, its
comfort and joy

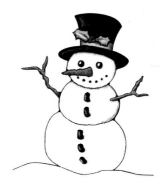

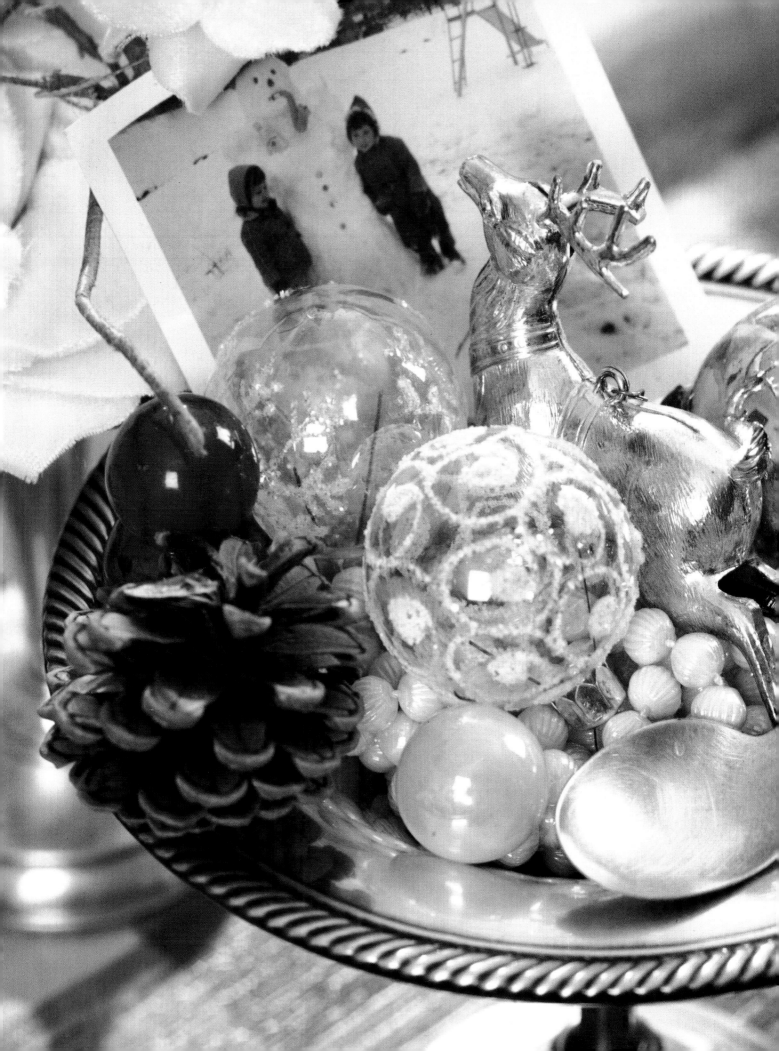

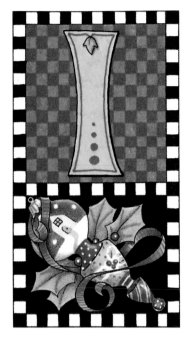

magine celebrating Christmas without memories of Christmases past. What an impossible thought! The very first ornament you lift from the box each December is guaranteed to connect you to those earlier celebrations. All of us carry in our hearts traditions that we reenact, pass along, and adapt as our lives change. We all have stories and keepsakes of Christmas that evoke a grin, a sigh, a laugh. How lucky we are for the links to the gaiety we've known, the people we've loved. Christmas cheerfully carries us back; it asks only that we bring along the best of ourselves: gratitude, humor, and love. In the rush of the season, we carry this legacy with us; each year, we help it grow. Happy memories to you and your entire family.

CHRISTMAS PAST LAUNCHES CHRISTMAS PRESENT

THEY ARE HANDLED WITH exquisite care, just twice a year. First they are gently revealed beneath their wraps of tissue and newspaper, to thrill and delight us all just as they do every December. We'll adore them through the holiday celebration and then, with great care, pack them away for eleven months before their next appearance. All that work for such brief enjoyment? Yes, absolutely, because even though these baubles share our rooms for only a few weeks, they delight us and they reunite us with earlier generations. These trinkets are worth much more than silver and gold; they have the value of comfort and joy.

It's often said that the way we decorate our homes reveals a great deal about us, and so does our approach to holiday decorating.

In a Kansas City home, one family's traditional, opulent furniture and accessories are complemented by their massive collections of vintage pieces: German Santa figurines, Della Robbia wreaths; delicate birds with spun glass tails; ropes and ropes of glass beads; fragile figurine Christmas lights, and bottle-brush trees too numerous to count.

Though thousands of items in the collection are put into play each Christmas, this isn't a rigid and precise parade of treasures. The fun is in new groupings, some formal and carefully configured, others so casual they include glass ornaments displayed right in their original cardboard boxes, complete with their own vintage graphics and artwork. In this palace of plenty, sunlight filters in through multipane windows to glisten on golden peacocks, vintage trees lush with

TAKE A FAUX SHORT-CUT TO TRADITION

Now that the children are grown, with homes of their own, the massive tree that used to fill the living room isn't needed anymore. Taking its place is an elegant artificial tree erected on a table, dressed with the family's lavish decorations so the familiar comfort of the holiday is intact. With the extended family comes a longer shopping list; the table offers a safe holding place for all those gifts.

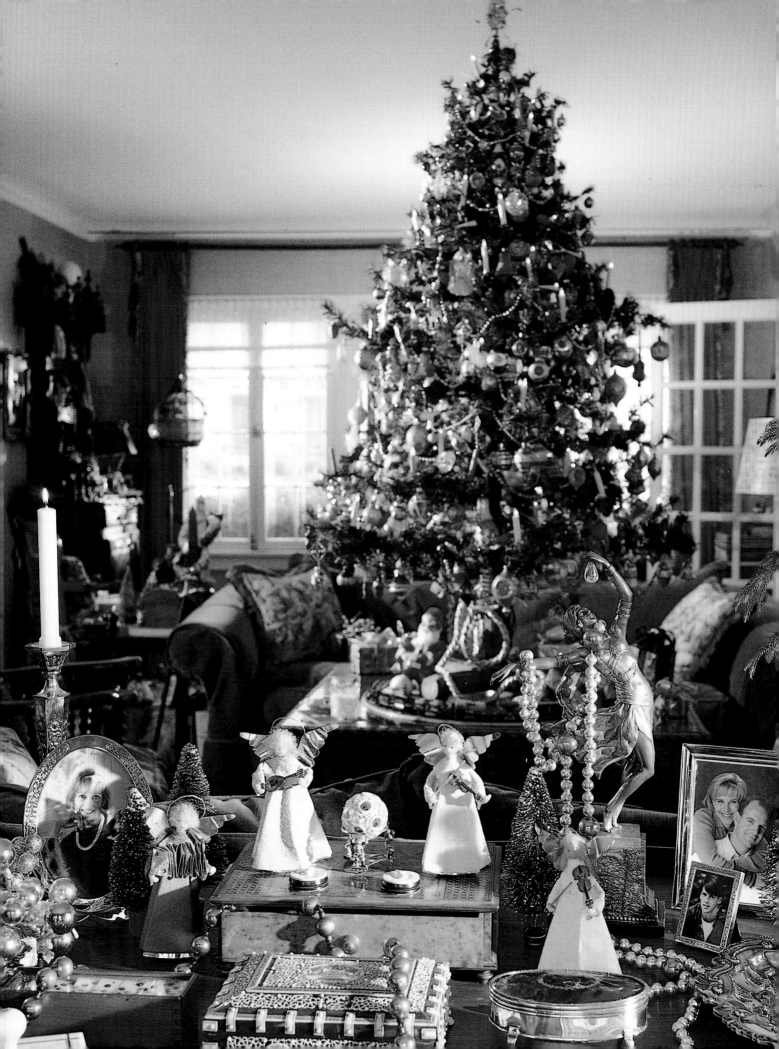

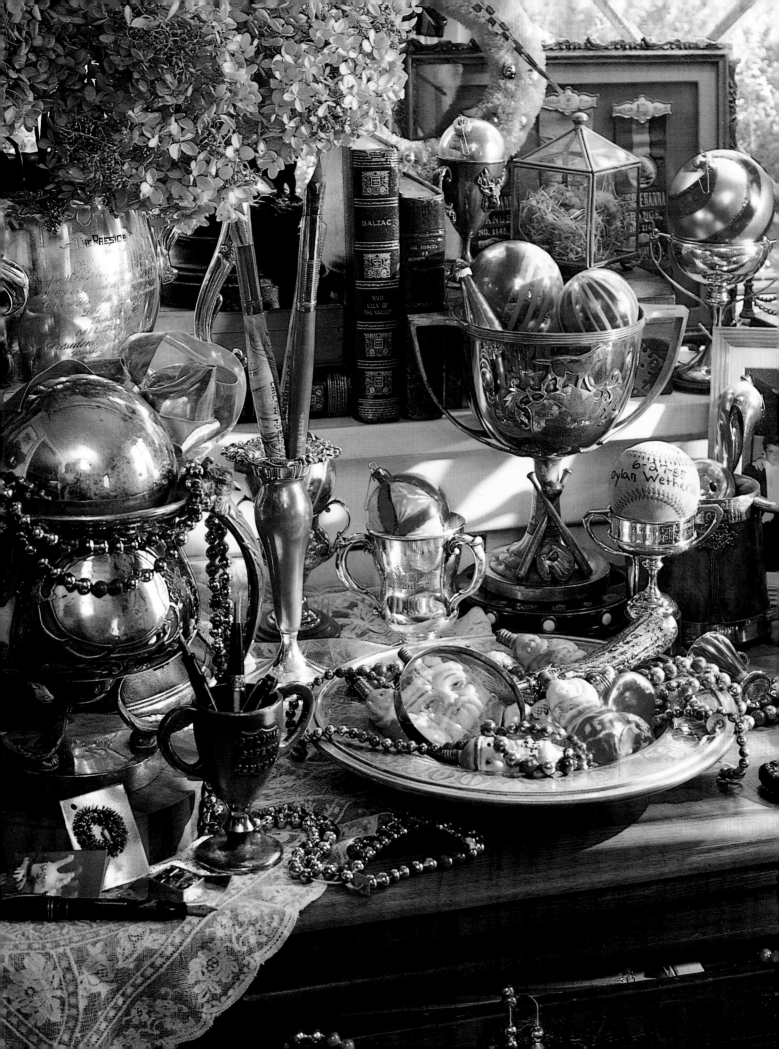

the tiniest ornaments, and a mechanical Christmas puppet hung from a coat hook. Angels are everywhere: on bookcases, a desk, even library tables. Little wreaths grace the candelabra; bellpulls are wreathed as well. A fresh ingredient each year is ribbon—spools and spools of rich, wide, double-face satin that's made into bows for sconces, chandeliers, lampshades, frames, and wreaths.

Throughout the home, before the decorations are unwrapped, the setting is prepared: Silverware is polished to gleam in sun and candlelight alike; crystal sparkles; wood glows. New, seasonal candles of all types are called into play: In the dining rooms, the chandelier will feature identical green ones; in the breakfast room, a candelabrum is fitted with six very different candle styles. Once the days of decorating are completed, family and friends can revel in a home that shares its generations of celebration.

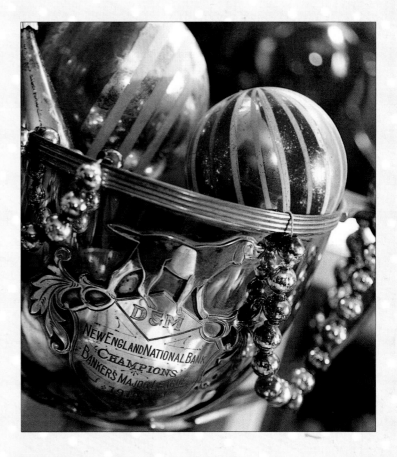

A HOLIDAY FOR THE LIBRARY

So many beautiful pieces, so little space. Luckily, this homeowner's philosophy of holiday happiness is to let the decorations spill over, be random, be amusing. Bring out the odd old trophies, silver sugar bowls, pewter pitchers, and silver plates. Pile them with ornaments as they come to hand, and include a few silly treasures, like a favorite autographed baseball. Here is a safe spot to display vintage ornaments in their campy original cartons, too. Taking over a loving cup (how appropriate) is an assortment of wonderfully muted striped ornaments; strings of glass beads loop over and around it. The gently tarnished sheen of cup, ornaments, and beads makes it all look as if it had been together forever.

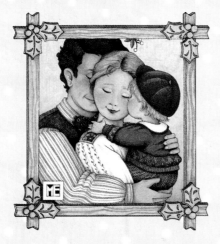

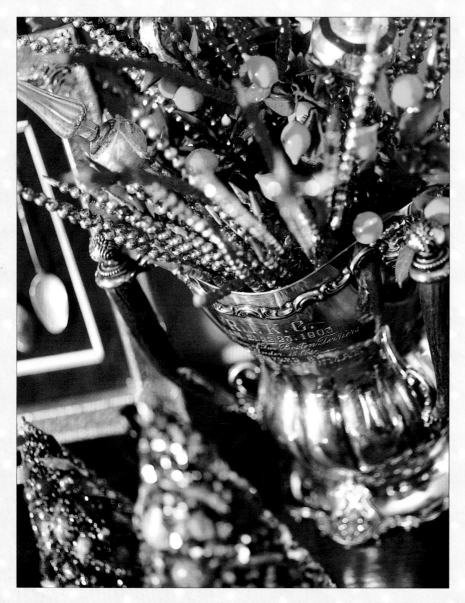

Treasures warm us through winter's chill, echoing Christmases through generations of a family.

ORNAMENTS NOWHERE NEAR A TREE

When you come across a sweet vintage ornament at a flea market or in a little shop, you may decide to pass on the purchase because you don't see it in your decorating plans for the holidays. If you like it, buy it. After all, every collection starts with one piece. Some spot in the house will catch your eye and you'll say, "Ah, yes, that's just the place!"

BE PLAYFUL IN A FORMAL ROOM

The culinary high point of the holiday season is Christmas dinner. Out come the finest linens, the ancestral china, crystal, and silver. Yes, it's lovely and comforting, but consider delighting your guests with decorations they absolutely won't expect. Instead of stolid reverence, create atmosphere with whimsical touches: An ornate gold frame is hung empty; within it is a round mirror crowned with a bouquet of ornaments. A community of goofy gnomes hangs from a sophisticated crystal chandelier, under a swag of sheer golden ribbon. The candlesticks on the table are bewreathed, and antique trees and too many Santas to count seem to be waiting for their dinner, too.

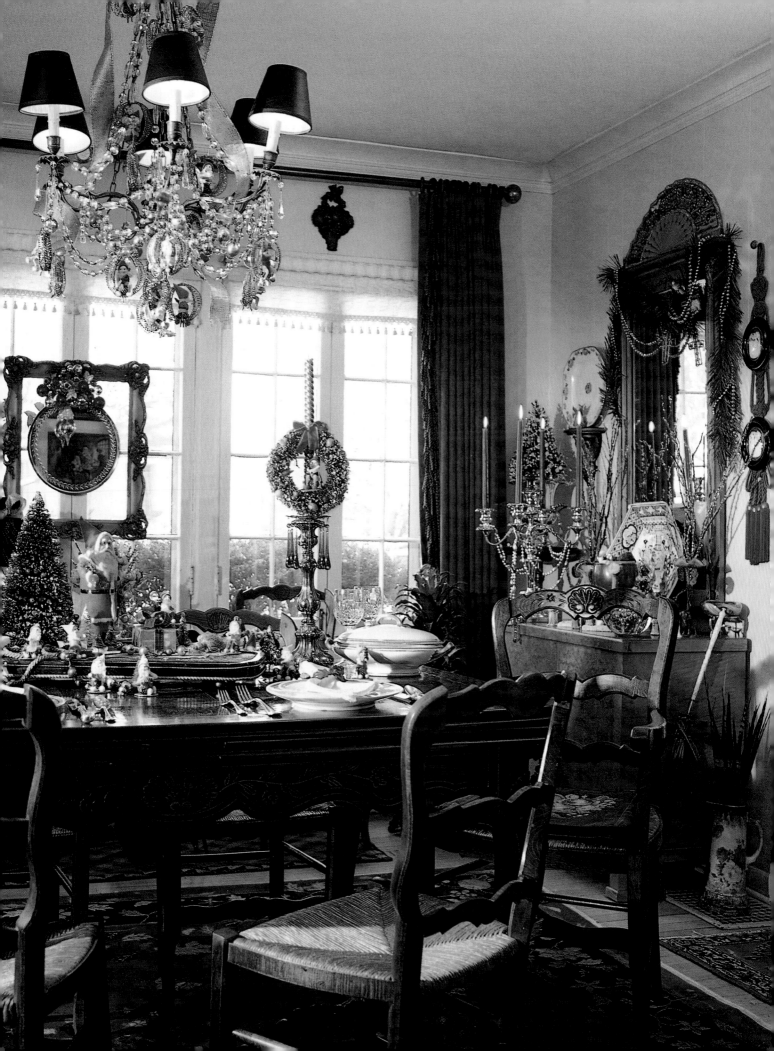

Memories

THE THRILL OF CHRISTMAS IS one of my earliest, most vivid memories. How filled every day was with preparations: the shopping, the list-making, the decorating, the cooking and baking. I never quite felt that I could remember it all, but my drawings and Christmas books were constant companions, along with the secrets and whispers: "Do you know what I got for so-and-so?" Far more entrancing than any birthday, far longer lasting, Christmas was the hands-down highlight of the year. Even school was better, with Christmas plays and grab-bags, and of course vacation! My sisters, Alexa and Peggy, and I were drawn closer during the excitement of the holiday, a trio of tireless collaborators stealthily pooling money, exploring shops, debating which was the perfect present for Pop or which surprise Mom would love most. Indeed, December was the month of the best behavior in our home, great pains being taken to please Santa Claus, who (we fervently believed) was especially interested in the comportment of the Engelbreit girls.

Christmas for me was rich artistic inspiration: angels; puppies in the snow; round-faced girls in holiday dresses (somehow they all bore an uncanny resemblance to my sisters and me); happy, package-laden shoppers. The most exquisite day of all, really, was not December 25th, but Christmas Eve: the rush to finish wrapping, the speculation about what the next day would hold; the final decorations on the tree; the moment when my sisters and I solemnly hung our empty stockings.

We grudgingly went off to bed for what would be the longest night of the year. "Are you asleep yet?" "Are you awake yet?" At dawn, we crept downstairs, Peggy always first, Alexa in the middle, and me last. Did our parents look sleep-starved and bleary-eyed? In the excitement we never really noticed. After our childhood, Christmas was never again as magical, until we became parents. And then we got the greatest gift: We became sleep-starved and bleary-eyed as our children gave Christmas back to us.

Mary

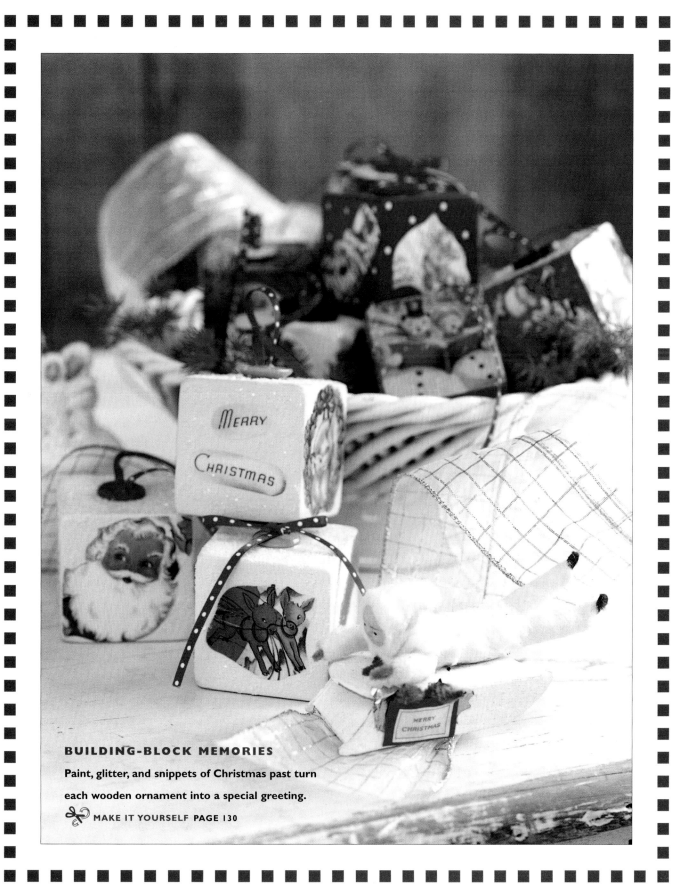

BUILDING-BLOCK MEMORIES

Paint, glitter, and snippets of Christmas past turn each wooden ornament into a special greeting.

✂ MAKE IT YOURSELF PAGE 130

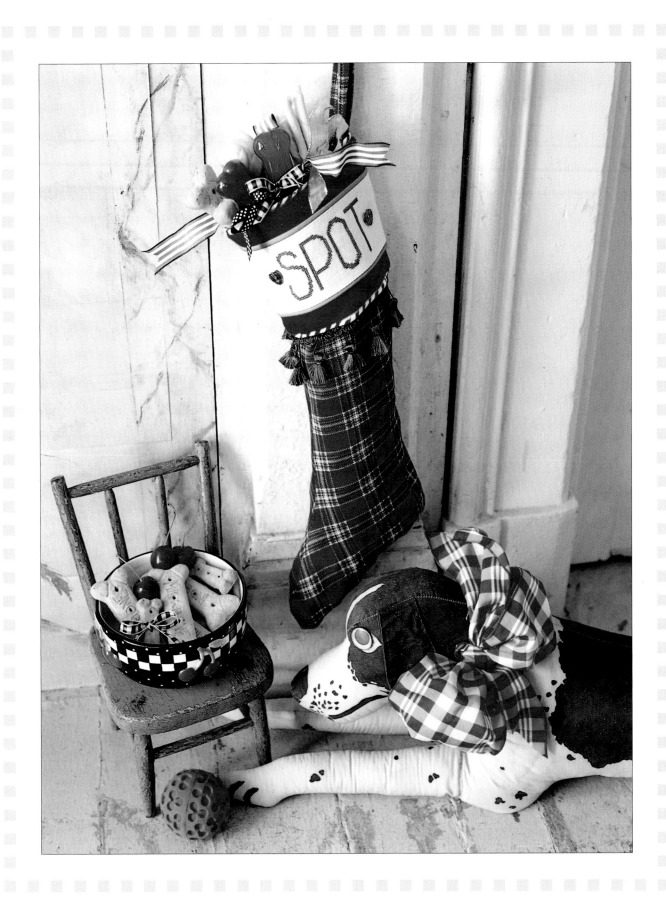

DOG DAY CHRISTMAS

Your dog probably wants to be spoiled with a really good present. But try as they may, dogs cannot write letters to Santa. Create a little Christmas for your pup in his favorite spot, which is either the kitchen floor or, when you're not home, the sofa. Hang his stocking low, put out a bowl of biscuits, give him a new stitched friend to tussle with. Since dogs like tradition too (they call it routine), sew up a stocking that Santa will fill year after year: To a plaid base, add fringe and stitch his name on the collar. It's a dog's life!

MAKE IT YOURSELF **PAGE 131**

A BEST FRIEND'S STOCKING

If you have friends' dogs on your Christmas list, make up stockings just for Fido, Spot, Rosie, Chloe, and Chester. Personalize each with a photo of the lucky pet and attach a dog tag with the name. Give the stockings wide tops to allow the dogs to retrieve every goodie. Fill stockings with biscuits, chews, rubber balls, and at least one annoying squeaky toy that will drive the master crazy. Nestle treats loosely in tissue paper so your dog can unwrap presents like everyone else in the family.

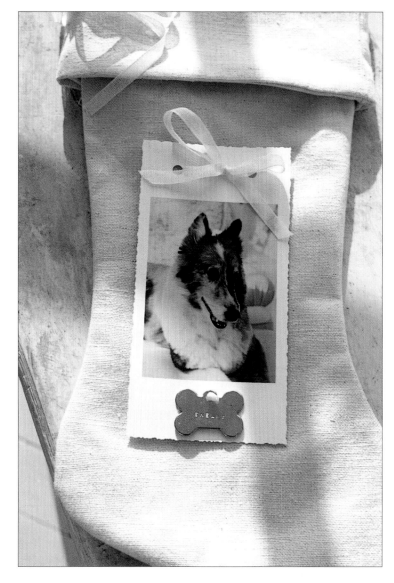

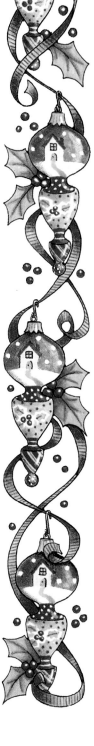

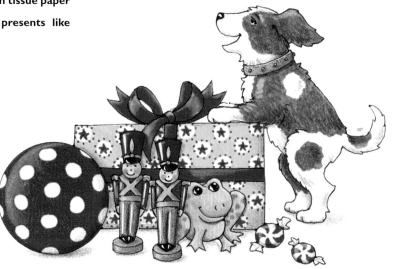

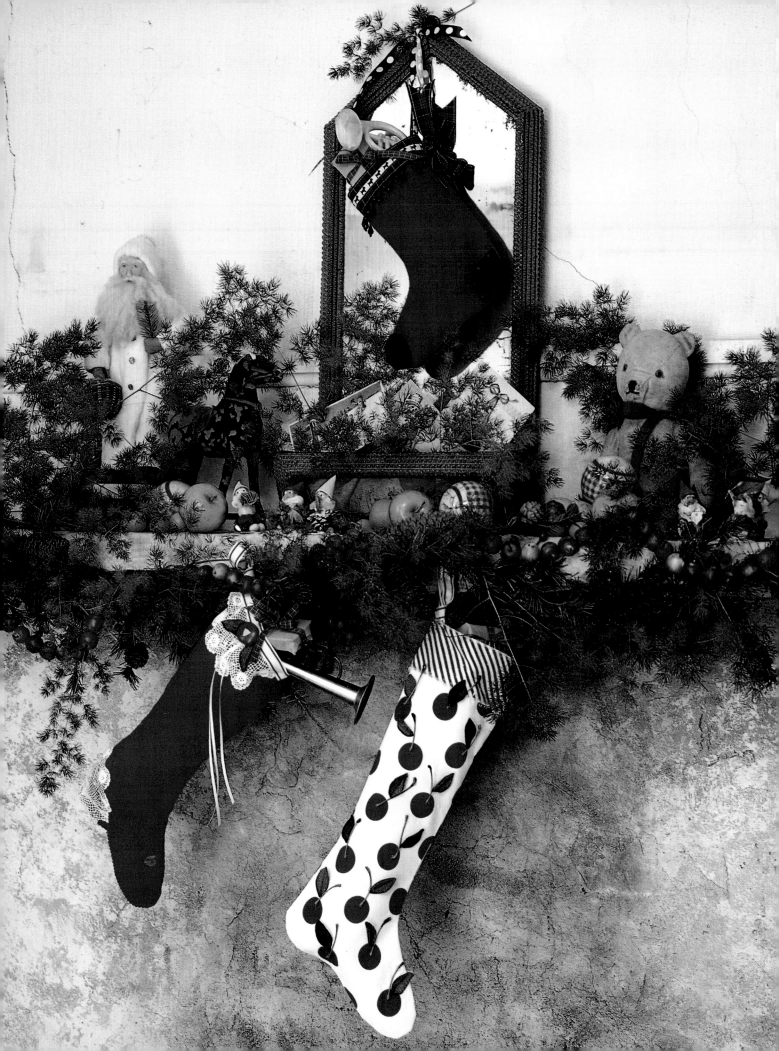

STOCKING COUTURE

The first ones may have been loopy old knit socks too worn for wear, but today's stockings are as chic as can be. Give your stockings character, too. For the cheerful trio, pair a crochet doily with red corduroy; red and black felt with Scottie and plaid ribbons; and red-and-white polka dots with candy-cane stripe ribbon.

Think of other combinations: velvet, cashmere, and satin; or hefty wools and corduroys; crisp cottons, canvases, and linens; or really girly lace, moiré, and organza. Create something beautiful from a favorite piece that may have some damage—a 1950s cotton tablecloth, a satin bedspread, a barkcloth slipcover. But what size? Make a teeny-tiny stocking for a pair of pearl earrings; stitch loose pearls outside to give a hint of what lies within. Sew up a long, skinny stocking for a pair of skis. Most stockings have cuffs of some kind—ribbon, contrasting fabric, lace, or bows. Mark the heels and toes with contrasting fabric. Delve into your jewelry box for loose beads of jet or crystal. Poke around the closet for pieces of millinery trim on hats you no longer wear. Now is the time, too, to raid the sewing box for buttons, bits of ball fringe, lengths of silk cord, and tassels. For the men in your family, sports insignias work every time. Finally, overstuff the stockings to tantalize the lucky recipients.

✂ MAKE IT YOURSELF **PAGE 132 & 133**

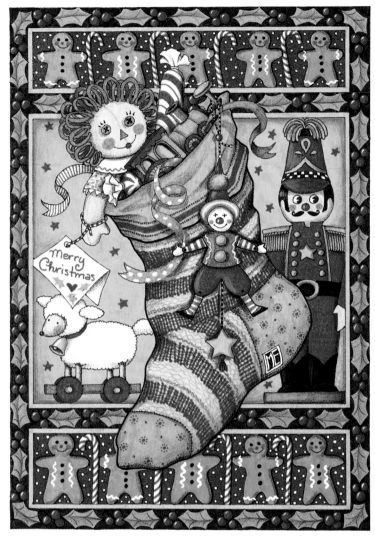

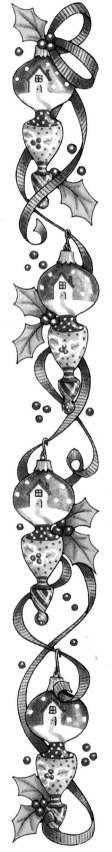

THE TEN ALL-TIME BEST
STOCKING STUFFERS

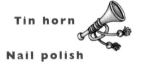

Tin horn

Rag doll

Nail polish

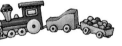

Jawbreakers

Robot

Peppermint sticks

Train engine

Penlight

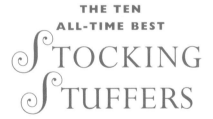

Spinning top

Marbles

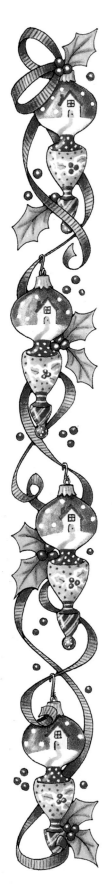

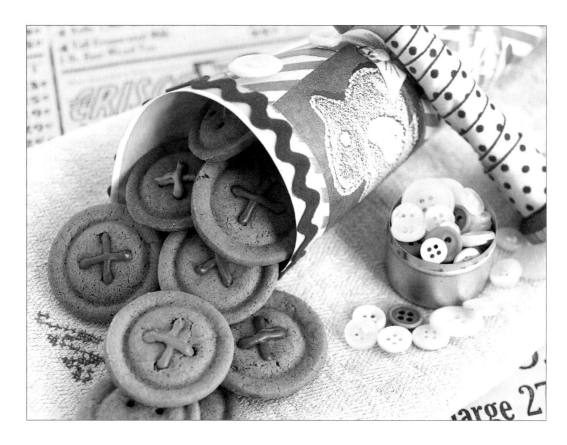

The best things come in the best packages.

OH, CHRISTMAS CONE

Who isn't fascinated by old magazines, with their wonderful advertisements and graphics. These gift cones were inspired by a stack of vintage holiday issues from the 1950s whose bindings had come loose. Form a page into a cone, add some rickrack, and run buttons down the seam. They are a most original way to give favors, small presents, or a mix of homemade treats. Place the tiniest items at the bottom of the cones and build the gift with a variety of shapes, sizes, and embellishments. For a gift of cookies, line a magazine cone with waxed paper. The lining will keep the cone pristine, and one cone will hold just enough gingerbread buttons to keep a few children very content. Because they are quickly put together and undeniably witty, the cones are great fun to make and just as much fun to receive; they'll be keepsakes of a very special Christmas.

✂ MAKE IT YOURSELF ⭐ PAGE 110

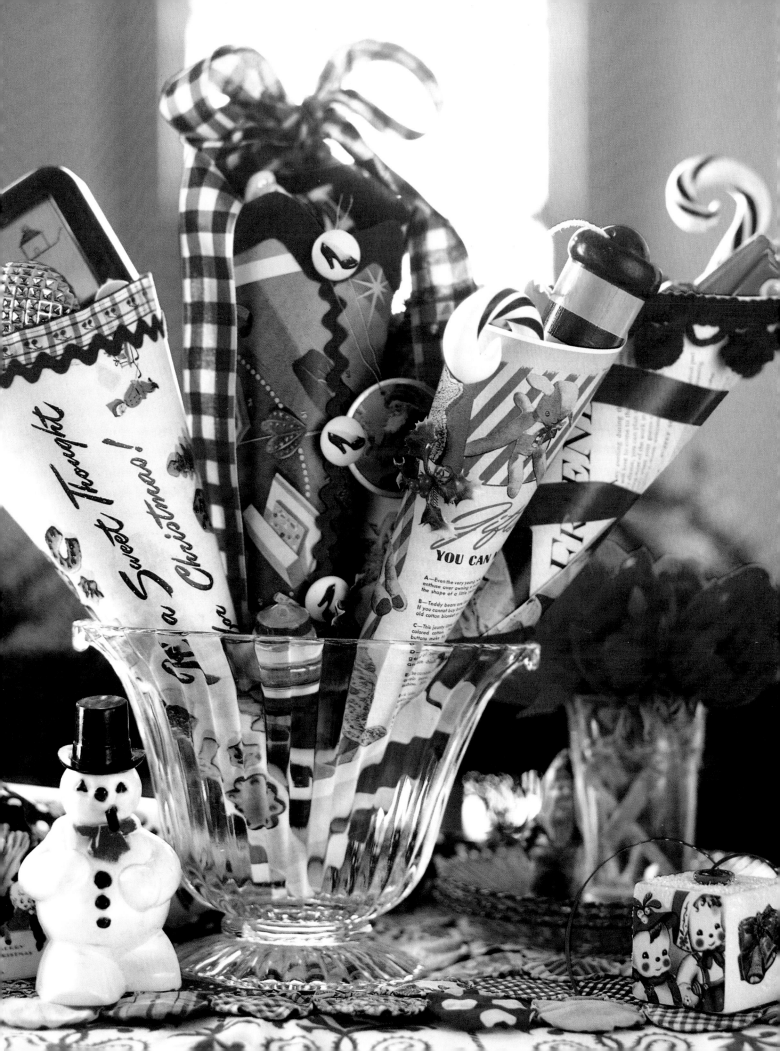

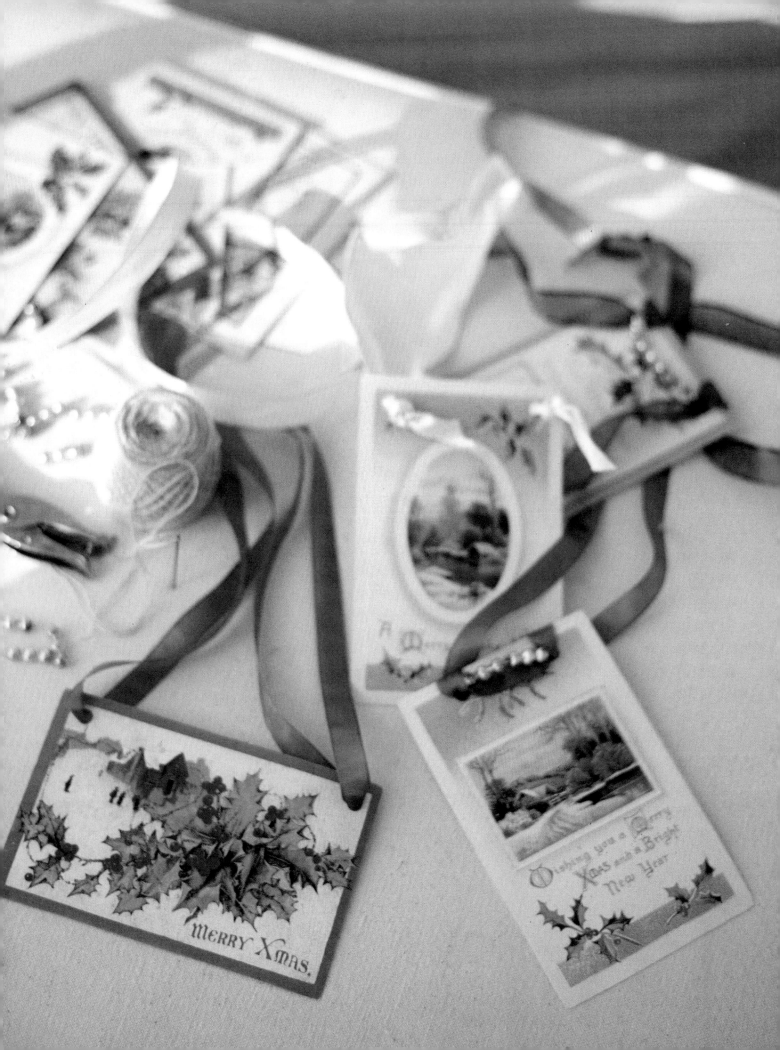

NEW LIFE FOR THE EARLIEST GREETINGS

The first printed Christmas cards were often postcards, with greetings and artwork on one side and an address and a personal note on the other. Today, they're easy to find for collectors, and thanks to color copiers, you can bring cards into your decorative schemes without damaging them. Have your favorites photocopied on heavy paper. Punch two holes in the tops, then loop lengths of ribbon through the holes, and tie the ends into bows. Hang them from doorknobs throughout the house to welcome callers. If you want to experiment, try silk thread, cotton cord, or raffia in place of ribbon. With thread, string on some loose pearls; for cord, some wood beads; and on the ribbon, jingle bells.

These are creative favors, too. Hang them from chair backs and let each guest take one home. Print the images on card stock and they become place cards. Have some reduced to smaller sizes for napkin rings or gift tags; enlarge them to turn them into gift wrap. Store the originals for safekeeping or frame them to hang in the powder room or to display on a bedside table in the guest room.

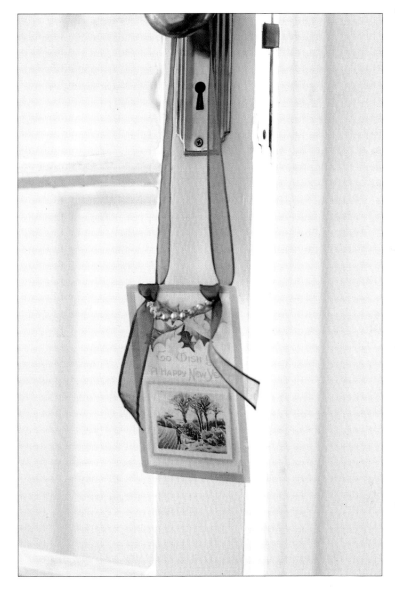

Every Christmas card wishes you holiday happiness over and over again.

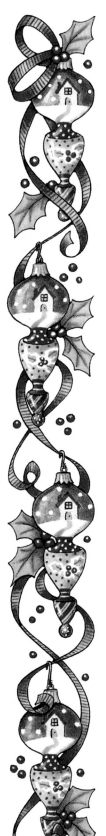

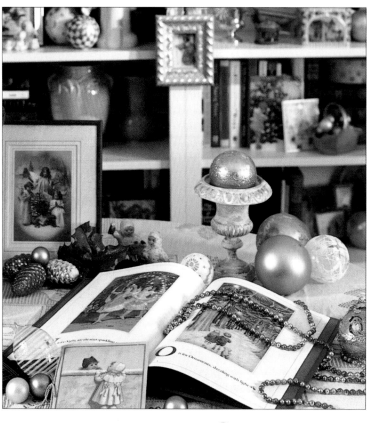

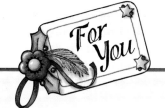

CHRISTMAS AT MARY'S

No matter what room you're in, you'll find a tribute to the holiday. A longtime collector of antiquarian Christmas books, Mary loves to display different volumes throughout the season. Surrounding the books are framed cards, strings of glass beads, and a seemingly random collection of bulbs (actually, they all share a gold-silver-copper-brass palette).

THE SPLENDOR OF THE SEASON

Our beloved Christmas ornaments—they're the jewels of the season, the stars of the celebration. Even when they're aged and their dazzling colors have turned smoky with tarnish, they're still beautiful. Gather them up and create a glorious, one-of-a-kind wreath. Examine and lightly dust the bulbs; arrange them loosely in a circle with the shapes evenly balanced. With a glue gun, fix the bulbs to a plain wreath base, beginning with the least interesting ones. Keep adding bulbs, putting their best faces forward.

For You

No time to put together an heirloom wreath? **Pile your ornaments** *in a wooden wine crate, a silver punch bowl, or a brass planter. Nestle them in greenery on the mantel.* **Hang them from a garland.**

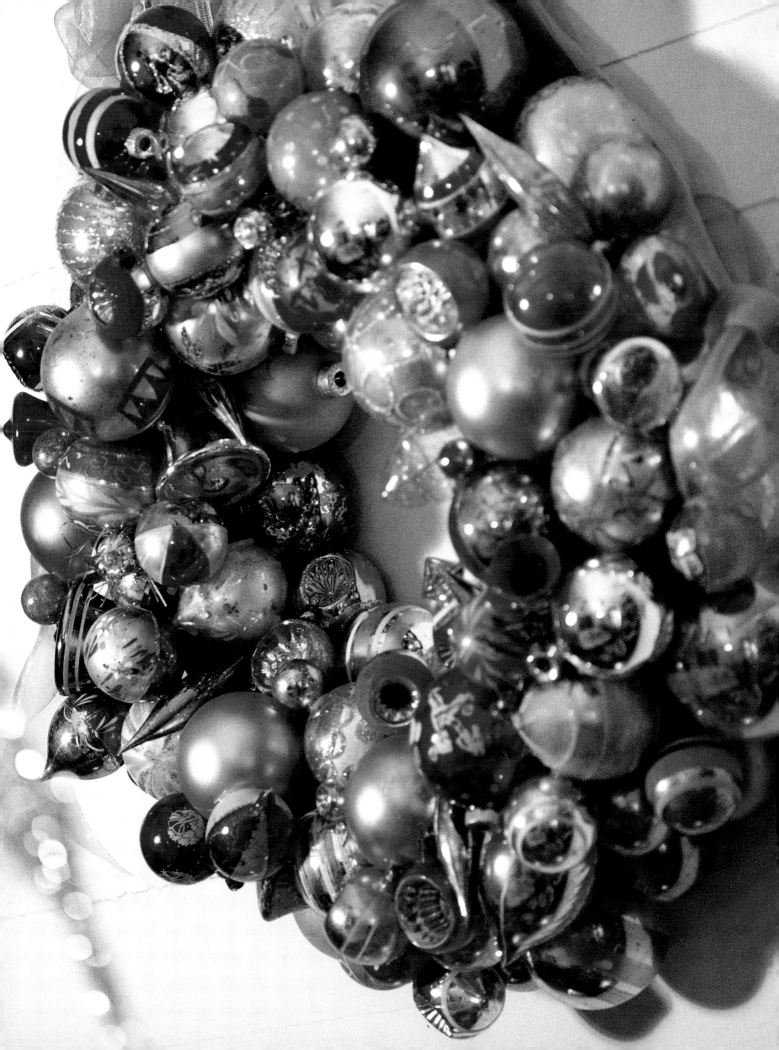

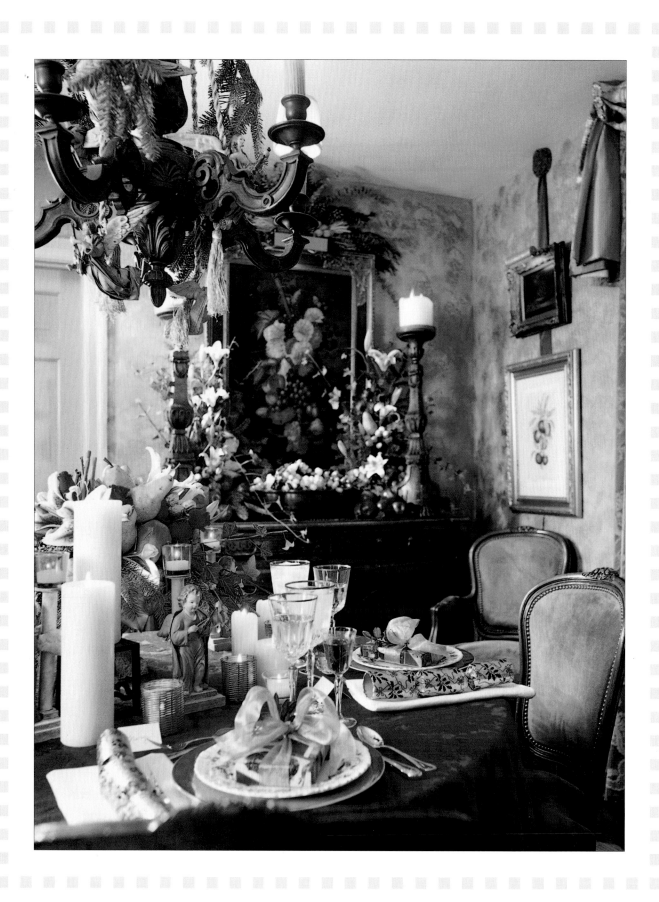

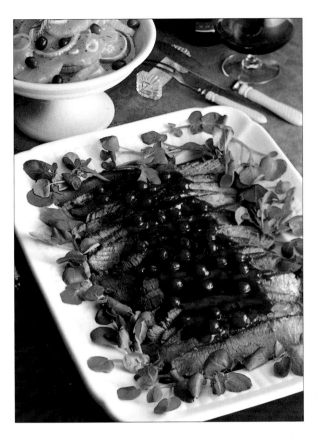

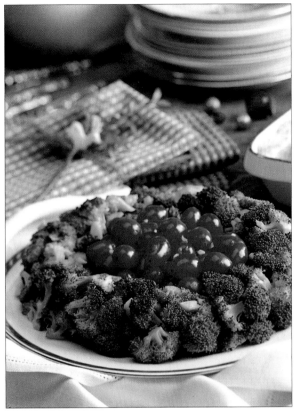

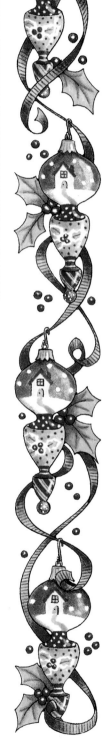

A GIFT THAT'S ALWAYS
IN GOOD TASTE

Dinner on Christmas day: Why shouldn't it be just as much fun as every other part of the celebration? Begin with a table set for a good time. Toss a rich red velvet cloth over the table, and lay out all your lovely china and stemware. Instead of formal candelabras, create a lush scenario at the center of the table. You might begin with a vase of heavenly lilies, and then add lots of fat pillar candles of different heights and votives in skinny glass stem holders. Make sure a golden cherub faces each diner. Set a wrapped gift on every plate, and don't forget the Christmas crackers—this is one meal you'll want to start off with a bang!

CHRISTMAS DINNER
IS SERVED

Holiday menus are often considered sacred, but there may be good reason this is the only time of year we endure boiled onions, mashed turnips, and sweet potatoes with marshmallows. Be revered as a Queen of the Kitchen by presenting tantalizing surprises. What does your family really love? In this case, it's brisket. Add something special to make it sing, such as the cranberries included here. You must have vegetables, so create a stunning presentation: a broccoli wreath with cherry tomatoes! It's emphatically Christmas in appearance, and it's delicious, simple, and healthful.

🥣 MAKE IT YOURSELF **PAGES 112 & 113**

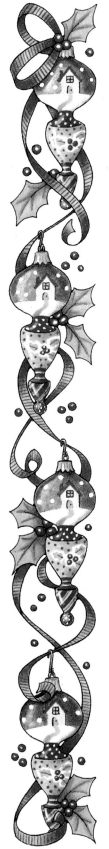

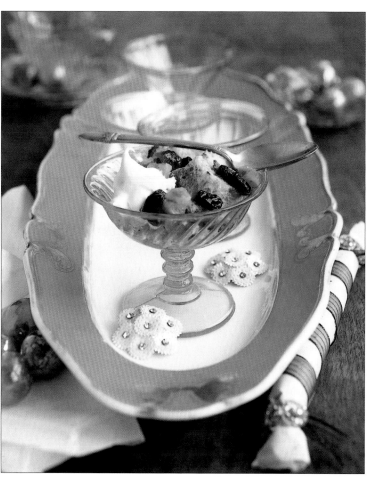

CHRISTMAS PUDDING PAST AND PRESENT

Christmas pudding in England is a serious affair—a combination of dried fruits, brandy, and molasses, and sometimes even suet—that's steamed for hours. (America's notorious fruitcake is really a second cousin of the mother country's dessert.) Here is a reinvented Christmas pudding for modern palates, made with traditional fruitcake ingredients but kept as light as falling snow. Serve this soft, sweet comfort food on your favorite holiday dessert plates or in brightly colored Depression glass sherbet bowls.

MAKE IT YOURSELF PAGE 115

PASS THE FAVORS, PLEASE

Clear the table. It's time for dessert. But first, let's all enjoy one last gift. Choose small favors and wrap each in paper. Tie them in ribbon and attach a Christmas tree pin to each bow. Popular since the 1950s, tree pins twinkle with tiny jewel ornaments; Grandmother always wore one on her winter coat. They make wonderful curtain tie-backs, napkin holders, and advent calendar decorations.

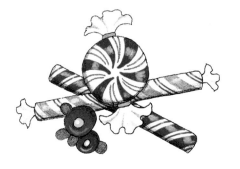

Blessed by Christmas sunshine,
our natures, perhaps long leafless,
bring forth new love, new kindness,
new mercy, new compassion.

—HELEN KELLER

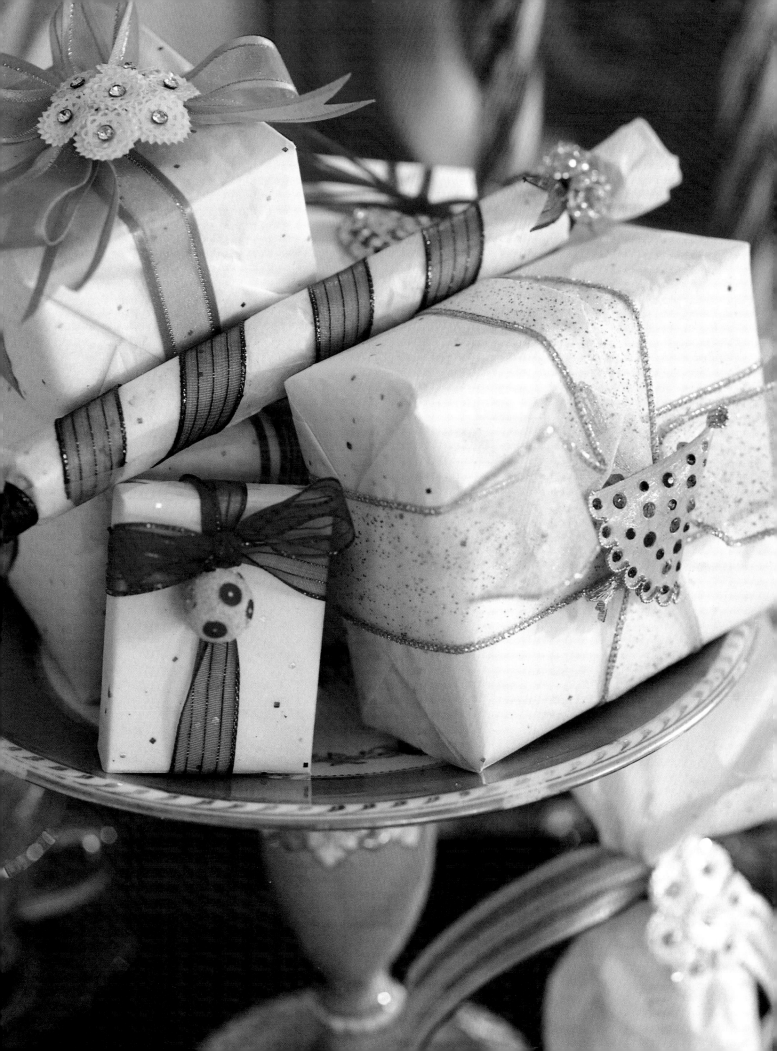

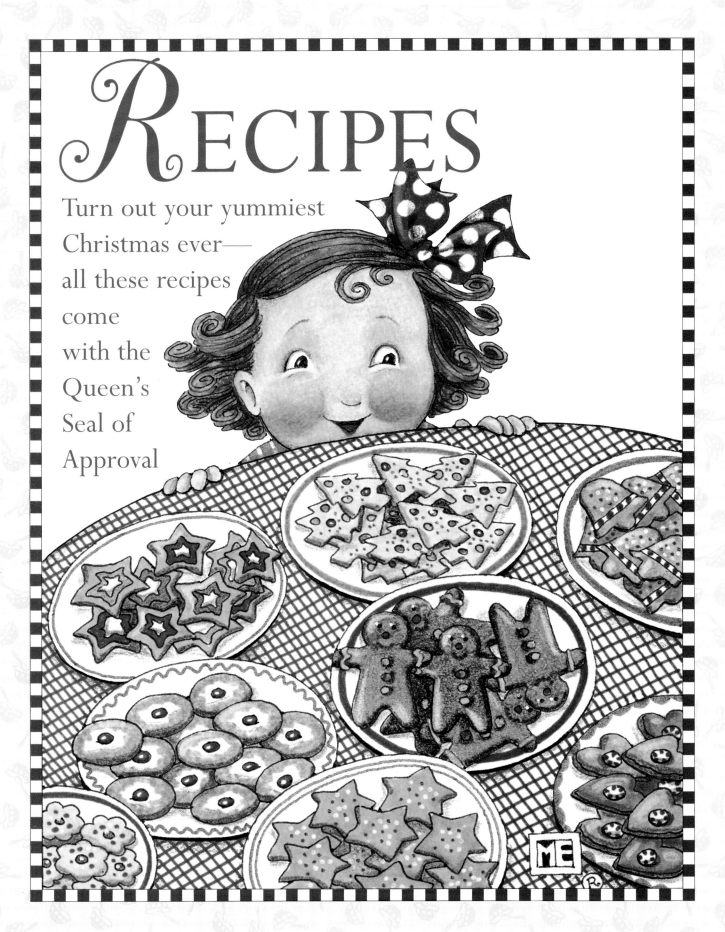

RECIPES

Turn out your yummiest Christmas ever—all these recipes come with the Queen's Seal of Approval

Poppy-Blue Cheese Straws

SKIP THE CHEESE PLATTER; INSTEAD, give your holiday cocktail party extra crunch with these delectable straws. For a special treat, try one of the new cow's or goat's milk blue cheeses made by American artisan cheese makers, available in gourmet shops.

    2 tablespoons poppy seeds
    2 teaspoons coarse salt
    One 17.25-ounce package frozen puff pastry,
        thawed
    Generous ½ cup crumbled blue cheese
    1 large egg, lightly beaten

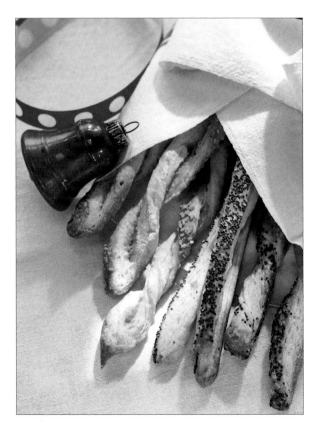

1. Preheat the oven to 425°F.

2. In a small bowl, combine the poppy seeds and salt; set aside.

3. On a lightly floured surface, unfold 1 puff pastry sheet. Roll the pastry sheet to a ⅛-inch thickness. Sprinkle half the blue cheese over half the pastry sheet, leaving a ½-inch border along the edges. Fold the pastry sheet half without cheese over the half with cheese and pinch the edges to seal. Roll the pastry to a ¼-inch thickness. Brush the top with some of the egg and sprinkle with half the poppy seed mixture.

4. Remove the edges of the pastry sheet to even it. Cut the pastry sheet lengthwise into ½-inch-wide strips. Twist each strip 4 or 5 times, if desired, and place ¾ inch apart on ungreased heavy baking sheets, gently pressing down on the ends of each strip to keep it twisted. If you are baking the pastry in batches, refrigerate unbaked straws.

5. Bake the straws for 12 to 14 minutes, or until they are golden brown and crisp. Transfer the straws to a wire rack to cool completely. Bake the remaining straws chilled, directly from the refrigerator.

Makes about 1½ dozen straws

 NO SHORT STRAWS
Tuck cheese straws into folded napkins or gather them in vintage hankies knotted in saucy bows. They also look enticing standing in a vase, in a reed or wire basket, and even in pitchers.

Garlic-Sesame Straws

U NEXPECTED GUESTS ARE TO BE expected at this time of year, so keep easy nibbles like this on hand. A study in contrasts, these straws combine a crunchy outside with a delectably sweet caramelized garlic interior. Leave them flat or twist them into swirls before baking.

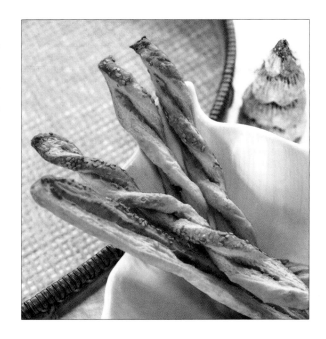

> 2 whole garlic bulbs, unpeeled
> 1 tablespoon oil
> 2¼ teaspoons coarse salt
> ⅛ teaspoon freshly ground pepper
> 1 tablespoon sesame seeds
> One 17.25-ounce package frozen puff pastry,
>   thawed
> 1 large egg, lightly beaten

1. Preheat the oven to 400°F. With a sharp knife, slice off the top quarter of the garlic. Place garlic on a sheet of foil large enough to enclose it. Drizzle with oil and sprinkle with ¼ teaspoon salt and the pepper. Seal the foil and bake 45 minutes, or until the garlic is caramelized. Remove from the oven and let cool.

2. Gently squeeze the garlic out of its skin into a small bowl; discard the skins. Using a fork, mash the garlic to form a smooth paste; set aside.

3. In another small bowl, combine the sesame seeds and 2 teaspoons salt; set aside.

4. Preheat the oven to 425°F. On a lightly floured surface, unfold 1 puff pastry sheet. Roll the pastry sheet to a ⅛-inch thickness. Spread half the garlic paste over half the pastry sheet, leaving a 1-inch border along the edges. Fold the bare half over the half with the garlic paste and pinch the edges to seal. Brush the top with some of the beaten egg and sprinkle with half the sesame seed mixture.

5. Remove the edges of the pastry to even it out. Cut the pastry lengthwise into ½-inch-wide strips. Twist each strip 4 or 5 times, if desired, and place ¾ inch apart on ungreased heavy baking sheets, gently pressing down on the ends of each strip to keep it twisted. If you are baking the pastry in batches, refrigerate unbaked straws.

6. Bake the straws for 12 to 14 minutes, or until golden brown and crisp. Transfer to a wire rack to cool. Bake the remaining straws chilled, directly from the refrigerator.

Makes about 1½ dozen straws

Herb-Crusted Pecans

C HRISTMAS AFTERNOON, WHEN all the presents have been opened and the kids are out with their new sleds, have some nibbles on hand as you listen to holiday music. Serve these flavored nuts in a McCoy planter or in some Swanky Swig glasses. You might also toss the nuts into a salad of winter greens like radicchio, chicory, and endive. Another possibility: Chop the nuts and roll cheddar cheese balls in them.

4 teaspoons dried dill

1 ½ teaspoons dried basil

½ teaspoon salt

2 tablespoons olive oil

3 cups pecan halves

1. Preheat the oven to 250°F.

2. In a mini food processor, grind the dill and basil until finely chopped. Transfer to a large bowl, add the salt and oil, and stir to combine. Add the pecans and toss to coat completely.

3. Spread the nuts on an ungreased baking sheet and bake for 30 minutes. Cool completely on the pan, then transfer to a serving bowl.

Makes 3 cups

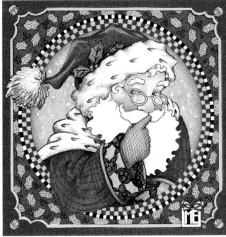

 SANTA AT THE OFFICE
Your colleagues at work will appreciate a gift of fancy nuts. Present them in wax paper sandwich bags that you've decorated with vintage postcards or recycled Christmas cards glued to their fronts. Punch two holes in the top of the bag and thread narrow polka-dot ribbon through to close.

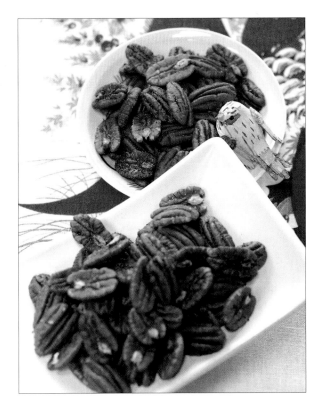

Spicy Honey Almonds

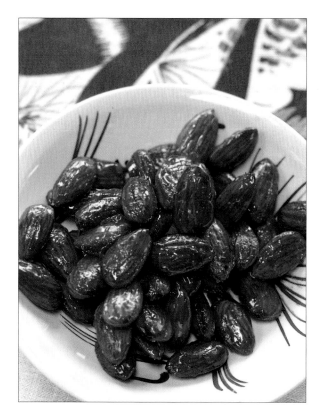

COUNT THE NUMBER OF GUESTS you'll have and how many of these enticing nuts you think they'll eat—then double that amount. They're always wildly popular! For the best flavor, make them a day ahead. Their playful nip staves off hunger during tree trimming parties. This is a recipe that's easy to double or triple.

1/2 cup honey

1 1/2 teaspoons ground ginger

1 teaspoon ground red pepper

1/2 teaspoon salt

3 cups unblanched whole almonds

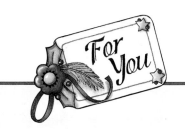

Give yourself a little break this year. First, **draw up the list** *of dinners, desserts, and treats to prepare, then take a deep breath and* **cross off at least five** *recipes. You know you always make too much anyway.*

1. Preheat the oven to 250°F. Generously oil a heavy baking sheet.

2. In a small saucepan over medium heat, heat the honey just until very runny; remove from the heat. Add the ginger, ground red pepper, and salt, and stir to combine. Add the almonds and, with tongs, toss to coat evenly and completely. Spread the almonds on the prepared baking sheet and bake for 1 hour, tossing once or twice during the baking.

3. Let the almonds cool completely on the baking sheet. Break them into small clusters and place them in serving dishes.

Makes 3 cups

Chocolate-Chestnut Truffles

PREPARE YOURSELF FOR A MOST delightful interlude—this is a decadent treat that's chocolate through and through. These truffles are wonderful after dinner, served with a snifter of brandy or a demitasse of espresso. Since they're bite-size, they'll satisfy chocolate cravings while curbing overindulgence. Make them with the best-quality ingredients you can find.

One 16-ounce can whole chestnuts

6 ounces bittersweet chocolate,
    coarsely chopped

6 tablespoons (¾ stick) unsalted butter,
    at room temperature

½ cup sugar

2½ tablespoons brandy

1 teaspoon vanilla extract

14 ounces semisweet chocolate,
    coarsely chopped

½ cup Dutch-process cocoa powder

1. Drain the chestnuts and pass them through a potato ricer set over a medium bowl; set aside.

2. In a double boiler over gently simmering water, melt the bittersweet chocolate; let cool slightly.

3. In a medium bowl with an electric mixer at medium speed, cream the butter and sugar together until fluffy. Add the chestnuts, brandy, and vanilla, and blend well. Stir in the cooled chocolate until well combined. Chill the mixture until it is set.

4. With a melon baller, roll the mixture into 1½-inch balls. Set the truffles on an ungreased baking sheet. If the mixture becomes too soft, chill in the refrigerator for a few minutes. Refrigerate the truffles for 10 minutes.

5. In a double boiler over gently simmering water, melt the semisweet chocolate; let cool slightly. With a fork, carefully immerse each truffle in the melted chocolate, then place it on a rack over wax paper. Allow to set for several minutes. Dust the truffles with cocoa before serving.

Makes about 5 dozen truffles

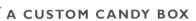

A CUSTOM CANDY BOX

Present truffles in fluted paper cups (available at candy supply stores) and arranged in a single layer in an airtight tin. Decoupage the tin with color copies of vintage cards or cookbook art.

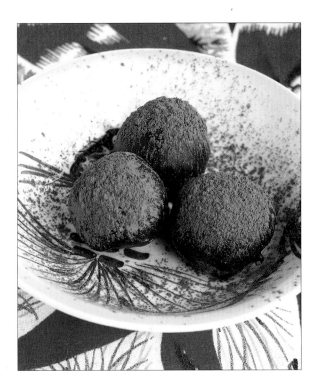

Bûche de Noël

BÛCHE DE NOËL IS SO RETRO, it's classic. This is the ultimate finale to Christmas dinner. For a snow-topped log, the completed cake can be dusted with sifted confectioners' sugar.

CHOCOLATE CURLS

½ pound semisweet chocolate, coarsely chopped

CHOCOLATE CAKE

⅔ cup all-purpose flour

⅓ cup unsweetened cocoa

Pinch of salt

6 large eggs, at room temperature

1 cup granulated sugar

3 tablespoons unsalted butter, melted

1 teaspoon vanilla extract

½ cup confectioners' sugar

BUTTER GANACHE

1 pound semisweet chocolate

1 ½ cups heavy cream

6 tablespoons (¾ stick) unsalted butter, cold

1 ½ cups heavy cream

¼ cup kirsch

Strawberries, for garnish

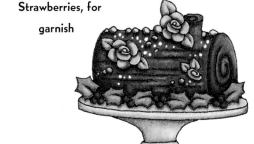

1. Make the chocolate curls: In a double boiler over gently simmering water, melt the chocolate. With a metal pastry scraper, spread the chocolate out on the back of an ungreased baking sheet about ⅛ inch thick. Chill in the refrigerator for 20 minutes.

2. Let the chocolate stand at room temperature for 1 to 2 minutes to soften slightly. With a clean pastry scraper, scrape the chocolate into curls. The curls are not meant to be the same size and shape, but to resemble bark. If the chocolate becomes too warm, chill in the refrigerator for a few minutes. Refrigerate the curls until ready to use.

3. Prepare the chocolate cake: Preheat the oven to 350°F. Set a saucepan one third full of water to simmer. Lightly butter and flour an 11½- by 15½-inch jelly-roll pan.

4. In a medium bowl, sift together the flour, cocoa, and salt 3 times; set aside.

5. In a large bowl with an electric mixer at low speed, beat together the eggs and granulated sugar. Place the bowl over the simmering water—the bowl should not touch the water—and continue beating until the mixture is lukewarm and the sugar has almost dissolved, 3 to 4 minutes. Test with your finger to gauge the warmth and the smoothness of the mixture. Remove from the heat.

6. With the mixer at high speed, beat the egg mixture until it becomes pale and thick, 2 to 3 minutes. The mixture is sufficiently beaten when it falls in a thick ribbon from a rubber spatula and sits on the batter for several seconds before sinking.

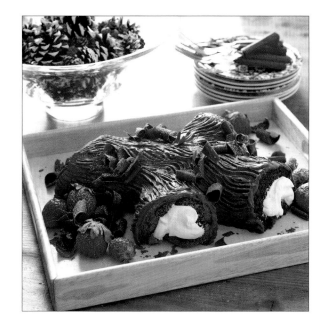

7. With a rubber spatula, gently and quickly fold the flour mixture into the batter one third at a time. Fold only until the flour is incorporated. Add the butter and vanilla, folding only until the liquids are distributed throughout the batter.

8. Pour the batter into the prepared pan, smooth the top, and bake in the center of the oven for 15 to 20 minutes, or until a toothpick inserted in the center comes out clean.

9. Cool the cake on a wire rack for 10 minutes. Sprinkle a kitchen towel or parchment paper with some confectioners' sugar in a rectangle 1 or 2 inches wider than the cake. Turn the warm cake out onto the towel and sprinkle with additional confectioners' sugar. Starting from a longer side, roll up the cake fairly tightly, using the towel for support. Set the rolled cake aside, wrapped in the towel, to cool completely.

10. Prepare the butter ganache: Chop the chocolate into matchstick-size pieces and place them in a large mixing bowl.

11. Bring the cream to a boil. Immediately pour the cream onto the chopped chocolate and let sit for 1 minute. Stir until smooth. Strain through a medium sieve set over a bowl; discard the solids.

12. Stir the butter 1 tablespoon at a time into the chocolate mixture, until each piece has melted before adding the next; set aside.

13. In a large bowl with an electric mixer at medium-high speed, beat the 1½ cups cream until just barely firm. Unroll the cake and sprinkle it with kirsch. With a metal spatula, spread with whipped cream. Gently reroll the cake, seam side down, and refrigerate for about 15 minutes.

14. With a serrated knife, diagonally slice off about one third of the roll. Cut this smaller piece diagonally in half to form 2 angled pieces or "stumps."

15. Transfer the largest piece of cake to a serving plate; frost it, except for the ends, with the ganache, reserving about ½ cup for the stumps. Position a stump on each side of the cake. Press gently to secure them in place. Refrigerate the cake again for about 15 minutes.

16. Frost the stumps, except for the ends, with the reserved ganache. Drag the tines of a large fork along the ganache to resemble bark.

17. Place the chocolate curls on and around the cake. Add whipped cream to the ends of the cake. With your fingers and a small spatula, press the bark into the ganache. Garnish with strawberries.

Serves 8

Scottie & Ball Cookies

AS MUCH ABOUT DECORATING AS eating, these adorable cookies can look like anything you want them to: Cut them into Scotties, balls, stars, or Santa shapes—whatever is in your cookie cutter collection. If you want to bake with the kids, this is a good, solid recipe. One caution: Cookies hung on evergreen trees absorb the pine aroma and may pick up residual soil from the trees.

VANILLA COOKIES

5 cups all-purpose flour

4 teaspoons baking powder

¼ teaspoon salt

1 cup (2 sticks) unsalted butter,
    at room temperature

1 cup granulated sugar

4 large eggs

4 teaspoons vanilla extract

ROYAL ICING

1 box (1 pound) confectioners' sugar

3 tablespoons egg white powder

6 tablespoons water

Paste food coloring in black, red, and green

4-inch lengths of ribbon, optional

1. Make the cookies: In a large bowl, mix the flour, baking powder, and salt until combined; set aside.

2. In another large bowl with an electric mixer at medium speed, cream together the butter and granulated sugar. Beat in the eggs one at a time until combined. Beat in the vanilla.

3. Gradually add the flour mixture to the butter mixture and mix with a wooden spoon until combined. Divide the dough into 4 pieces, shape each piece into a disk, wrap in plastic, and refrigerate for 3 to 4 hours.

4. Preheat the oven to 350°F. On a lightly floured surface, using 1 disk at a time, roll the dough out to a ⅛-inch thickness. Cut into shapes using a 4-inch Scottie cutter and a 3½-inch round cutter. Place the dough on ungreased baking sheets 1 inch apart. If you intend to hang the cookies, use a small straw to pierce a hole in the top of each cookie wide enough for the ribbon. Gather the scraps and reroll to make more cookies.

5. Bake the cookies for 9 to 11 minutes, or until they are lightly browned. Check the holes to make sure

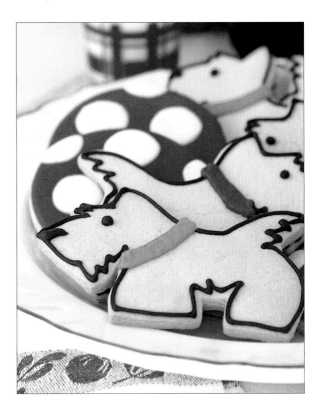

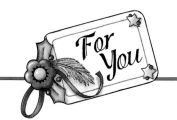

*Who doesn't love lots of **Christmas cookies**? Put aside a couple of days just for baking and set up an **assembly line**. Make the kitchen off-limits to everyone but bona fide helpers and watch your productivity soar.*

they are still intact; if not, poke them again. Transfer the cookies to a wire rack to cool.

6. Make the royal icing: In a large bowl with an electric mixer at medium-high speed, beat the sugar, egg white powder, and water until thick and fluffy, about 4 minutes.

7. Remove 1 cup of icing and set aside. Divide the remaining icing in half. Tint one half red. Divide the remaining icing in half again and tint one portion green and one portion black.

8. Fill a pastry bag fitted with a small plain tip with black icing and pipe a border around each Scottie. Add a nose and an eye to each. Fill pastry bags with some of the green and red icing and pipe the collars. Set aside to dry.

9. To decorate the ball cookies, fill a resealable plastic bag with some of the red icing. Snip a small corner from the bag and pipe an outline of the cookie around the edge. Thin the remaining red icing with water until it is easily spreadable. With a long metal spatula, cover the cookies with red icing. Allow to dry thoroughly, preferably overnight.

10. Thin the white icing with water. Dip a 1-inch round cutter into the icing and lightly imprint the red balls to outline the white dots. With a paint brush, fill in the white outlines with icing. Allow the icing to dry, about 1 hour.

11. If you like, string ribbons through the holes in the cookies and tie the ends into small bows. Hang the ornaments on the tree—or from anything else that catches your eye.

Makes about 3 dozen cookies

FOR ME?
YOU SHOULDN'T HAVE!

Sturdy Scottie cookies make unforgettable (and delicious) gift tags for those presents you'll be handing out personally. They're also fun as place cards at a kids' party. Rather than adding the dog's collar, pipe each name in red or green along the body of the Scottie. Hot Dog!

Oat & Hazelnut Shortbread

I**F THE SHORTBREAD YOU'VE HAD** before was store-bought, your tastebuds will flip over home-baked ones. Oats and hazelnuts make the texture and flavor of the shortbread a bit more interesting. Once baked, these are cut into wedges known as "petticoat tails" in Great Britain.

½ cup unblanched whole hazelnuts

½ cup rolled oats

10 tablespoons (1 ¼ sticks) unsalted butter,
     at room temperature

½ cup confectioners' sugar

3 tablespoons firmly packed dark brown sugar

1 teaspoon grated orange zest

⅛ teaspoon almond extract

1 cup all-purpose flour

¼ teaspoon salt

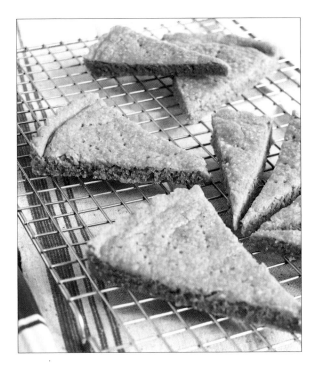

1. Preheat the oven to 400°F.

2. Spread the hazelnuts on an ungreased baking sheet and bake for about 7 minutes, or until they are lightly toasted. Transfer the nuts to a clean kitchen towel. Fold the towel over the nuts and rub vigorously to remove the skins. Set the nuts aside.

3. Spread the oats on the baking sheet and toast about 7 minutes, or until they are golden. Transfer the nuts and oats to a food processor and pulse until the mixture is finely ground. Reduce the oven temperature to 350°F.

4. In the large bowl of an electric mixer at medium speed, beat the butter with both sugars until light and fluffy. Beat in the hazelnut mixture, orange zest, and almond extract. Reduce the mixer speed to low; beat in the flour and salt until well blended.

5. Transfer the dough to an ungreased 9-inch round tart pan with a removable bottom. Place a sheet of waxed paper over the dough and, with your hands, press the dough evenly into the pan, smoothing the top. Remove the waxed paper and prick the dough all over with a fork. With a lightly floured knife, lightly score the dough around the inside rim, then score the dough deeply into 12 wedges.

6. Bake the shortbread about 20 minutes, or until it is firm to the touch. Set the pan on a wire rack to cool slightly. Recut the wedges to separate. Let them cool. Remove the sides of the pan and transfer the shortbread to a serving platter.

Makes 1 dozen shortbread wedges

Herb & Prosciutto Muffins

SIMPLE PLEASURE IS A GOOD description for these savory muffins. Full of down-to-earth-goodness, they beat out haute cuisine, even for Christmas. Make them in two sizes; smaller ones are good for anyone who has filled up on candy canes.

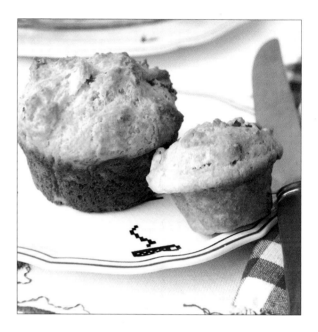

- **2 cups all-purpose flour**
- **2 teaspoons baking powder**
- **½ teaspoon baking soda**
- **¾ cup grated Parmesan cheese**
- **⅓ cup chopped thinly sliced prosciutto**
- **2 large eggs**
- **¾ cup milk**
- **½ cup sour cream**
- **¼ cup (½ stick) unsalted butter, melted**
- **I tablespoon honey**
- **I tablespoon olive oil**
- **½ medium onion, chopped**
- **I ½ teaspoons finely chopped fresh rosemary**
- **I teaspoon finely chopped fresh thyme**

1. Preheat the oven to 375°F. Generously grease a 12-cup muffin tin or a mini muffin tin, or line it with paper or foil baking cups.

2. Into a large bowl, sift together the flour, baking powder, and baking soda. Stir in the Parmesan and prosciutto; set aside.

3. In a medium bowl, combine the eggs, milk, sour cream, butter, honey, oil, onion, rosemary, and thyme, whisking until the mixture is combined. Pour the wet ingredients into the dry ones, stirring the batter only until it is just combined.

4. Spoon the batter into the prepared muffin pan cups, filling each about three quarters full.

5. Depending on their size, bake the muffins for 15 to 20 minutes, or until the tops spring back when lightly touched. Let the muffins cool in the tin for several minutes, then transfer to a wire rack to cool.

Makes 12 or 18 muffins

 BUTTERING UP GUESTS

Serve muffins and breads with aromatic herbed butters. Mix together I stick unsalted butter, softened, with 3 tablespoons finely chopped fresh parsley, tarragon, thyme, or basil and freshly ground pepper to taste. Roll the butter in wax paper to form a log and chill it until firm. Slice the log into rounds and fan out on a chilled serving plate.

Winter Breakfast Frittata

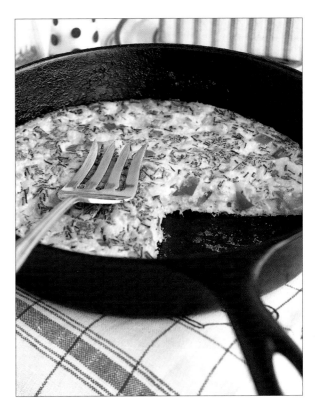

Y OU CAN TAKE ALL THE CREDIT for this frittata—so naturally festive with red and green peppers—anytime during the holiday. Enjoy it before heading off to bed on Christmas Eve, or as a delicious and healthful snack between all the rich foods of the two days. Frittata is so versatile; once it's cooled, cut it into thin slices and make sandwiches on French baguette, or cut it into strips and toss them into some fried rice.

> 2 tablespoons unsalted butter
> 1 medium onion, halved and sliced
> Salt, to taste
> 8 large eggs, beaten
> ¼ cup milk
> ¼ cup grated Parmesan cheese
> ½ cup chopped mozzarella
> 2 tablespoons chopped fresh chives
> ½ teaspoon freshly ground pepper
> ½ each red and green bell peppers, cored, seeded, and chopped

1. Preheat the oven to 350°F. Generously butter a deep 10-inch ovenproof skillet.

2. In a medium skillet over medium-low heat, melt the butter. Add the onion, season with salt, and sauté for 7 minutes, or until it is lightly golden. Remove from the heat and let cool slightly.

3. In a large bowl, combine the eggs, milk, cheeses, chives, ½ teaspoon salt, and the pepper, mixing well. Add the onion and peppers and stir gently to combine the ingredients.

4. Pour the mixture into the prepared skillet and bake for 30 minutes, or until it is golden brown on top and set in the middle. Remove from the oven and let cool on a wire rack for 5 minutes.

Serves 4 to 6

 MORNING MERRIMENT

Wake up to a breakfast table decorated with tiered cake stands brimming with kumquats, kiwis, clementines, starfruits, mangoes, papayas, baby bananas, and other tropical fruits. Nestle shiny ornaments in with the fruits and drape them with lengths of curly ribbon. At the place settings, tie mandarin-orange-colored ribbons around green napkins.

Berries & Pound Cake Parfait

Make pound cake from scratch, or buy one and skip ahead to the lemon cream recipe.

POUND CAKE

Scant 2 cups cake flour (not self-rising)

1 teaspoon baking powder

½ teaspoon salt

¾ cup (1 ½ sticks) unsalted butter, at
    room temperature

1 ½ cups sugar

4 large eggs

¼ cup milk

¼ cup pure maple syrup

1 teaspoon vanilla extract

½ teaspoon almond extract

LEMON CREAM

2 cups heavy cream

1 tablespoon sugar

½ teaspoon grated lemon zest

1 teaspoon lemon extract

2 cups mixed raspberries, blackberries,
    and hulled, sliced strawberries

Mint sprigs, for garnish

1. Make the pound cake: Preheat the oven to 325°F. Butter and flour a 4½- by 8-inch loaf pan.

2. Sift together the flour, baking powder, and salt. In the large bowl of an electric mixer at medium speed, cream the butter and sugar until fluffy. Add the eggs one at a time and beat until well combined.

3. In a bowl, combine the milk, syrup, and extracts. Add the flour mixture alternately with the milk mixture to the butter mixture, beginning and ending with the flour, mixing until just combined.

4. Gently scrape the batter into the prepared pan and bake for 1 hour, or until a toothpick inserted in the center comes out clean. Cool the cake in the pan on a rack for 10 minutes; remove the pan and cool the cake completely on the rack.

5. Make the lemon cream: In the large bowl of an electric mixer at medium-high speed, beat the cream and sugar until soft peaks form. Add the lemon zest and extract and beat until combined.

6. Slice the cake crosswise into ½-thick slices. With a 2-inch star-shaped cookie cutter, cut out stars. Lightly toast the stars in a toaster oven.

7. Spoon some cream into each bowl. Top with some berries, 2 cake stars, and a mint sprig.

Serves 6

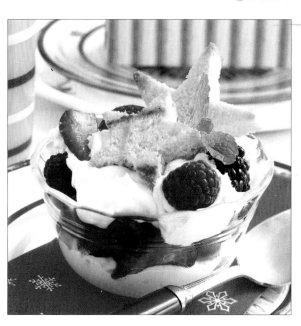

Apple-Oat Crisp

U NDER GOLDEN, CRUNCHY OATS and walnuts are succulently sweet and juicy apples. This is comfort food for the holidays at its best: quick and delicious. If you like, serve the crisp with Lemon Cream (page 107).

3 large Granny Smith apples, peeled, halved, cored, and sliced

2 cups rolled oats

½ cup firmly packed light brown sugar

½ cup chopped walnuts

½ cup raisins

½ teaspoon ground cinnamon

Pinch of freshly grated nutmeg

1 teaspoon vanilla extract

½ cup (1 stick) cold unsalted butter, cut into bits

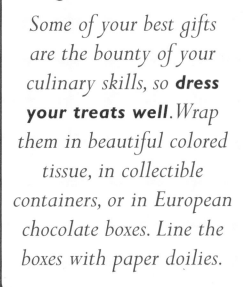

Some of your best gifts are the bounty of your culinary skills, so **dress your treats well**.*Wrap them in beautiful colored tissue, in collectible containers, or in European chocolate boxes. Line the boxes with paper doilies.*

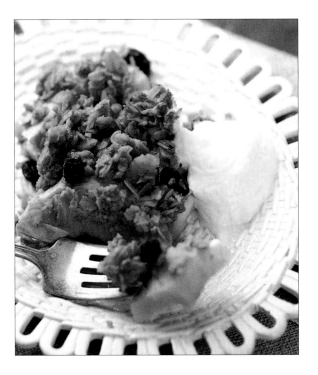

1. Preheat the oven to 350°F.

2. Arrange the apples in a deep-dish pie plate.

3. In a medium bowl, combine the oats, sugar, walnuts, raisins, cinnamon, nutmeg, and vanilla. With two knives or a pastry blender, combine with the butter until the mixture resembles a coarse meal. Sprinkle evenly over the apples.

4. Bake the crisp for 30 minutes, or until golden brown on top. Let the crisp cool on a wire rack for 10 minutes before serving.

Serves 6

French Apple Tart

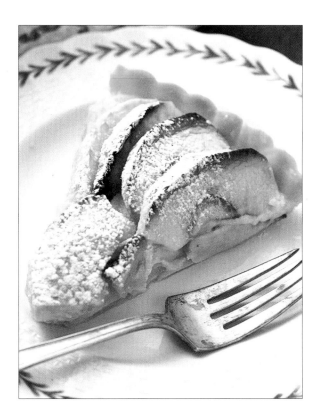

T HIS APPLE TART MAY BECOME one of your most beloved recipes. It's delicious, of course, plus it's a hardy traveler that will arrive at the party looking as festive as you do. You can also serve it when your family returns after midnight church services, or keep a tart on hand for drop-in guests. Back it up with a menu of Pumpkin-Leek Soup (page 111), a crisp tossed green salad, biscuits, and white wine.

> **Dough for a single-crust 9-inch pie, chilled**
>
> **3 large Granny Smith apples, peeled, halved, cored, and thinly sliced**
>
> **½ cup granulated sugar**
>
> **½ cup heavy cream**
>
> **1 large egg**
>
> **1 teaspoon vanilla extract**
>
> **Confectioners' sugar, for sprinkling**

1. Preheat the oven to 375°F.

2. On a lightly floured surface, roll the dough to a ⅛-inch-thick round. Transfer the dough to a 9-inch tart pan with a removable bottom and gently press it into the pan. Trim the overhanging dough. Chill the pastry in the pan for 30 minutes.

3. Arrange the apple slices in the pan in slightly overlapping concentric circles, starting on the outside and working toward the center. Bake the tart for 15 minutes.

4. Meanwhile, in a small bowl, whisk together the sugar, cream, egg, and vanilla. Pour over the apples and bake the tart for 25 minutes longer, or until the custard is set.

5. Cool the tart on a wire rack for 10 minutes. Remove the sides of the pan, sprinkle the tart with confectioners' sugar, and serve.

Serves 8

 KISS THE COOK

For the cook who has everything, make a customized apron. Purchase a plain canvas or twill apron from a housewares store, then launder it. Stencil on personalized motifs with colorful fabric paints. Let the paints dry completely, then wrap the apron with a wide red ribbon. Paint the top few inches of the handle of a plain wooden spoon to match the apron and tuck it into the ribbon.

Gingerbread Buttons

DON'T WORRY ABOUT POLITICAL correctness. Forget about gingerbread men and women, boys and girls. Just serve these one-shape-fits-all buttons.

2 cups all-purpose flour

2 ½ teaspoons ground ginger

1 teaspoon baking soda

1 teaspoon cinnamon

½ teaspoon ground cardamom

½ teaspoon ground cloves

¼ teaspoon salt

½ cup (1 stick) unsalted butter, at room temperature

1 cup firmly packed dark brown sugar

1 large egg

1 tablespoon light corn syrup

2 teaspoons vanilla extract

½ recipe Royal Icing (pages 102–103)

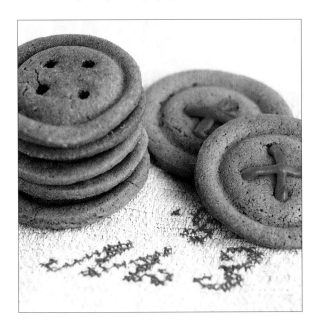

1. In a medium bowl, combine the flour, ginger, baking soda, cinnamon, cardamom, cloves, and salt; set aside.

2. In the large bowl of an electric mixer at medium speed, cream the butter and sugar until light and fluffy. Add the egg, corn syrup, and vanilla, and beat until well blended. Reduce the mixer speed to low and beat in the flour mixture until well blended. Divide the dough into 2 disks, wrap each in plastic, and refrigerate for at least 2 hours, or overnight.

3. Preheat the oven to 350°F. Butter 2 baking sheets or line with parchment paper.

4. Remove the dough from the refrigerator one half at a time, and let stand for 5 minutes. On a lightly floured surface, roll the dough out to a ⅛-inch thickness. With a 1½-inch round cookie cutter, cut out the dough. Place the cookies on the prepared baking sheets about 1 inch apart. With a 1¼-inch round cookie cutter, press a light indentation in each cookie, making sure not to go through. With a skewer, prick 4 holes in the center of each cookie to look like buttonholes. Gather the scraps and reroll to make more cookies.

5. Bake the cookies for 8 minutes, or until they are firm. Set the baking sheets on wire racks to cool for 1 minute. With a large spatula, transfer the cookies to the racks to cool completely.

6. With a pastry bag fitted with a small plain tip, pipe the royal icing to look like thread on each button. Let dry completely.

Makes about 4 dozen cookies

Pumpkin-Leek Soup

F EEL AS IF YOU'RE SLIPPING INTO a holi-daze? Regroup with this calming soup. (The pumpkin seeds have a satisfying crunch.)

2 tablespoons unsalted butter

2 medium leeks, white part only,
   thinly sliced and rinsed well

1 small onion, halved and finely chopped

4 cups ½-inch-dice pumpkin

4 to 6 cups chicken stock

Salt and freshly ground pepper

½ cup coarsely chopped toasted
   pumpkin seeds, for garnish

1. In a large pot, melt the butter over medium heat. Add the leeks and onion and cook, stirring often, for 10 minutes, or until the leeks are softened. Stir in the pumpkin and cook for 2 to 3 minutes, until it is coated with the butter. Pour in enough stock to cover by 1 inch. Increase the heat to high and bring to a boil. Reduce the heat to medium and simmer the mixture for 15 to 20 minutes, until the pumpkin is very tender.

2. In a food processor or blender, puree the soup in batches. Return the soup to the pot, reheat, and season to taste with salt and pepper. Ladle into bowls and sprinkle with the pumpkin seeds.

Serves 4 to 6

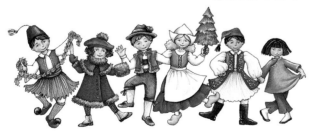

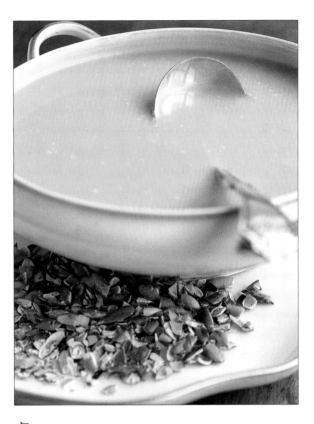

 SOUP'S ON

When you're hosting a holiday soup party, remember that soup is the great relaxer: Conversation flows, there's a lot of laughter, and you might even spot some elbows on the table! Have some choices simmering atop the stove—Pumpkin-Leek, a seafood chowder, beef-and-noodle, whatever your favorites are. Lay out "soup bar" garnishes, with freshly shaved Parmesan cheese, minced scallions, croutons, Garlic-Sesame Straws (page 96), salsa, sour cream, and toasted pine nuts.

Beef Brisket

T HIS YEAR, SURPRISE CHRISTMAS diners with their traditional beef tucked under a ruby cloak of cranberries. Start the dish the day before you want to serve it; after it cooks, it marinates a second time for a flavor wallop.

One 5-pound beef brisket
One 15-ounce bottle Italian salad dressing
1 cup firmly packed brown sugar
1 cup bottled barbecue sauce
1 cup fresh cranberries or whole cranberry sauce
Watercress or fresh parsley sprigs, for garnish

1. Place the brisket in a large baking dish, add the salad dressing, and turn to coat. Cover with plastic and marinate in the refrigerator for 3 to 4 hours, turning several times.

2. Preheat the oven to 300°F.

3. Remove the brisket from the marinade; discard the marinade. Wrap the brisket tightly in foil and place in a clean baking dish. Bake for 3½ hours.

4. Open up the foil and bake the brisket for 30 minutes more. Remove the brisket from the foil, reserving the juices. Place the brisket and the juices in a baking dish. Cover with plastic and refrigerate for 24 hours.

5. Preheat the oven to 300°F. Transfer the brisket to a cutting board. Drain the juices into a saucepan and add the sugar and barbecue sauce. Heat, over medium heat, stirring, until the sugar has dissolved.

6. Slice the brisket very thinly against the grain. Place the slices in a casserole and pour 1 cup of the

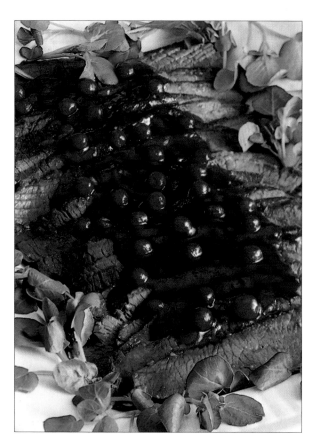

sauce over them. Cover the casserole with a lid or tightly with foil and bake for 1 hour.

7. Meanwhile, add the cranberries to the sauce remaining in the saucepan. Heat the mixture until the cranberries are soft but not mushy. Remove the sauce from the heat and set aside.

8. When the brisket is done, reheat the sauce. Arrange the meat on a serving platter and surround with watercress. Spoon the cranberry sauce over the brisket slices and serve.

Serves 12

Broccoli & Cherry Tomatoes

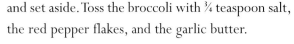

COLORFUL RED TOMATOES ARE ornaments surrounded by a ring of fresh broccoli in this edible Christmas wreath. The beauty of the wreath is that it looks so good your kids may not even notice you've slipped something truly healthful into them.

2 bunches (2¾ pounds) broccoli

3 tablespoons butter

1 garlic clove, pressed through a garlic press

Salt, to taste

Pinch of red pepper flakes

1 tablespoon olive oil

1 tablespoon
  chopped shallots

1 pint cherry or
  grape tomatoes

Freshly ground pepper

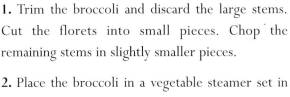

1. Trim the broccoli and discard the large stems. Cut the florets into small pieces. Chop the remaining stems in slightly smaller pieces.

2. Place the broccoli in a vegetable steamer set in a deep pot with boiling water. Steam, covered, for about 5 minutes, or until the broccoli is crisp-tender; be careful not to overcook. Immediately place the broccoli in a bowl of ice water to stop the cooking. When cold, drain and spin in a salad spinner to drain off as much water as possible. Let the broccoli sit a bit longer, then repeat the spinning until the broccoli is dry.

3. Meanwhile, melt the butter in a small skillet over low heat; stir in the garlic. Remove from the heat and set aside. Toss the broccoli with ¾ teaspoon salt, the red pepper flakes, and the garlic butter.

4. Firmly pack the broccoli into a 6-cup ring mold. Cover with foil and refrigerate.

5. Preheat the oven to 350°F. Place the broccoli in the oven and bake for 25 minutes.

6. Meanwhile, heat the oil in a small saucepan over medium heat. Add the shallots and sauté until wilted. Add the tomatoes and sauté for 1 minute, just to heat through. Season to taste with salt and pepper and remove from the heat.

7. Place a serving plate on the ring mold, carefully invert the mold and plate, and remove the mold. Replace any pieces of broccoli that don't cooperate. Spoon the cherry tomatoes into the center of the ring and serve.

Serves 8 to 10

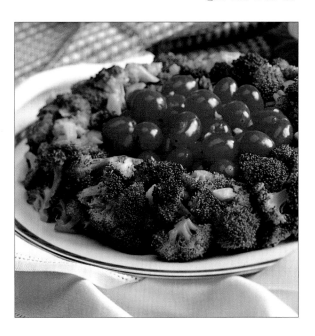

Red Cabbage with Cranberries

THINK OF THIS DISH AS THE frilly bow for your plate: The brilliant colors perk up any entrée. Simmering the berries in honey and apple juice eliminates the need for sugar—you're probably getting enough at this time of year already. Naturally, this goes well with any roasted meat or poultry, and it's a snap to make.

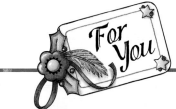

- 2 tablespoons unsalted butter
- 2 to 2 ½ pounds red cabbage, quartered, cored, and cut into ½-inch-wide strips
- 2 cups fresh cranberries
- 1 cup apple juice
- ¼ cup honey
- ¼ cup red wine vinegar
- ¾ teaspoon ground cardamom
- ½ teaspoon salt
- ¼ teaspoon freshly ground pepper

From the Queen of the Kitchen: **Always think of the palette as well as the palate.** *Put pizzazz in the colors of the menu—and choose serving dishes that would dazzle Picasso as well as Pepin.*

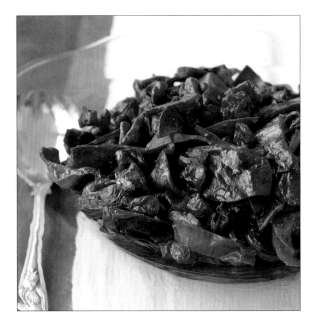

1. Preheat the oven to 350°F.

2. In a large heavy skillet over medium heat, melt half the butter. Add half the cabbage and sauté for 3 to 5 minutes, or until it is wilted. Transfer the cooked cabbage to a Dutch oven. Repeat with the remaining butter and cabbage.

3. Add the cranberries, juice, honey, vinegar, cardamom, salt, and pepper to the cabbage, and mix well to combine. Cover and bake for 45 minutes to 1 hour, or until the cabbage is tender; be careful not overcook. Transfer with tongs to a serving dish.

Serves 6 to 8

Mixed-Fruit Bread Pudding

A WINTER VERSION OF A FRESH fruit summer pudding, this dessert takes traditional fruitcake ingredients and gives them a light new twist. Serve it with whipped cream in footed glass dishes, Depression glass if you have them.

    ½ cup apple juice

    ½ cup raisins

    ¼ cup chopped pitted prunes

    ¼ cup chopped dried apricots

    ⅔ cup sugar

    8 slices (½-inch-thick) day-old sourdough bread,
        crusts removed

    3 tablespoons unsalted butter, melted

    2½ cups milk

    3 large eggs, lightly beaten

    2 teaspoons vanilla extract

1. In a small nonreactive saucepan, heat the juice until hot but not boiling. Add the raisins, prunes, and apricots; set aside to plump.

2. In a medium-size heavy skillet, cook the sugar over medium heat until it dissolves and turns a caramel color, stirring frequently. Carefully pour the caramel into a 9- by 13-inch pan and tilt to evenly coat the bottom.

3. Cover the bottom of the pan with the bread slices, tearing the bread as necessary to form a tight layer. Drizzle the bread evenly with the melted butter; set aside.

4. In a medium bowl, combine the milk, eggs, vanilla, and dried fruit with the juice, stirring to combine. Pour the mixture over the bread, using a spoon to distribute the fruit evenly over the top. Cover with foil and let stand at room temperature for 30 minutes.

5. Meanwhile, preheat the oven to 350°F.

6. Place the pan with the pudding into a larger baking pan in the oven. Fill the larger pan with hot water to come halfway up the sides of the smaller pan. Bake for 1 hour, or until set.

7. Let the bread pudding rest on a wire rack for about 10 minutes, then serve.

Serves 8

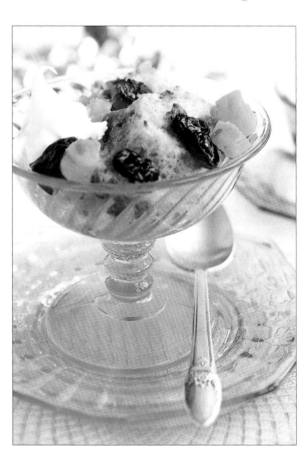

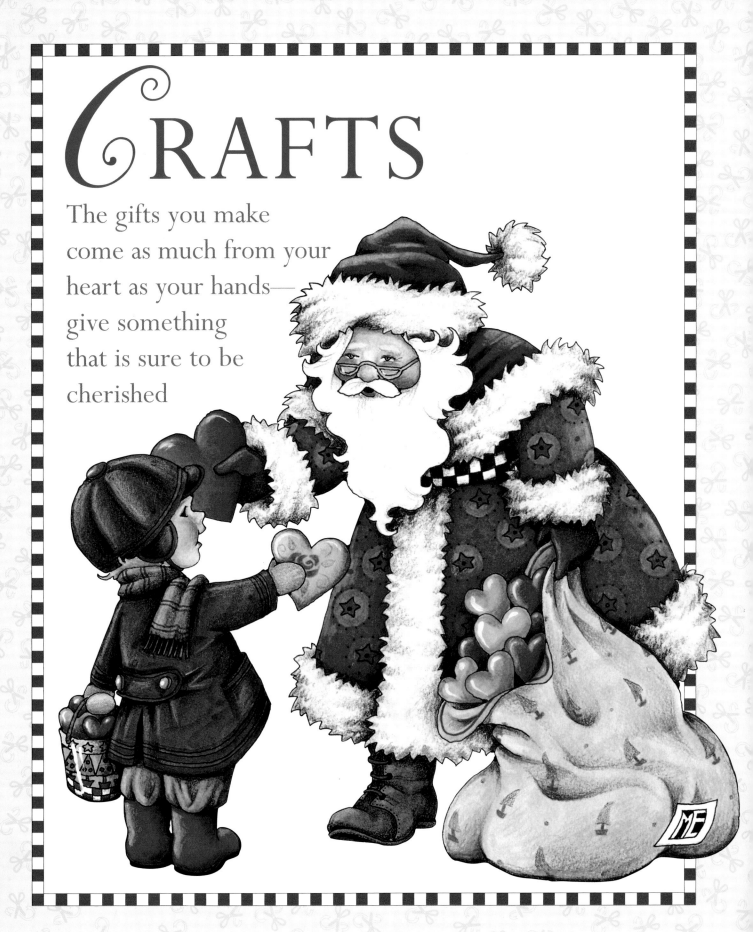

CRAFTS

The gifts you make come as much from your heart as your hands— give something that is sure to be cherished

The crafts in this book are not very complicated, but many do call for general sewing skills and equipment you probably already have at home. Listed below are the tools and supplies you'll need in addition to the specific materials listed for each project on the following pages. In addition to the basic stitches— a running stitch and a slip stitch, for example—there are two decorative embroidery stitches you'll need to employ; both are illustrated below. To make templates for the sewing projects, use the patterns on pages 135–139.

Your holiday sewing kit:

Sewing machine
Fabric shears
Pinking shears
Manicure scissors
Craft scissors
Hand-sewing needles
Sewing thread in Christmas colors
Embroidery floss in Christma's colors
#7 and #8 crewel needles
Straight pins
Craft knife
Fabric-marking pencil
Ruler and tape measure
Masking tape
Iron and ironing board

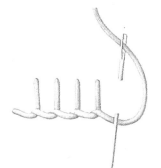

BLANKET STITCH

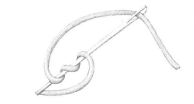

FRENCH KNOT

Advent Mittens

SHOWN ON PAGE 21

Make the anticipation as joyful as the celebration by hanging Advent mittens throughout the house. Fill each mitten with token treats and tiny toys, and open one per day, beginning on the first of December. You could also tuck in a Santa's helper message, like "Remember to fill the bird feeder" or "Send a Christmas card to someone who'd like to hear from you."

To make twenty-five mittens:

Mitten and numeral templates (page 135)

¾ yard 36"-wide red felt

¾ yard 36"-wide sage green felt

9" x 12" sheet black felt

3½ yards total ⅝"- to ⅞"-wide assorted plaid ribbons

5 yards ⅜"-wide dark green grosgrain ribbon

8 yards ⅛"-wide dark green double-faced satin ribbon

7 yards sage green piping

Fifty ⅝" red buttons

1 skein each red and sage green embroidery floss

1. Photocopy the mitten pattern at 100% and use it to trace and cut out 24 mitten panels from red felt and 26 panels from sage green felt. Use the ten numeral templates to cut the odd numbers 1 to 25 from red felt and the even numbers 2 to 24 from black felt. Lay out 25 of the mitten panels, alternating the colors (start and end with green). Place the felt numbers on them in sequence, red numbers on green mittens and black numbers on red mittens. Sew the numbers in place by hand.

2. For each numbered mitten, cut one 4½" length of plaid ribbon and two 4½" lengths of sage green piping. Position the ribbon across the mitten wrist, as indicated on the pattern. Tuck the piping under the ribbon edges and pin in place. Using a zipper foot, machine-stitch along the ribbon edges through all the layers. Fold the ends to the back, tack by hand, and trim away the excess.

3. Pair each numbered mitten panel with a plain mitten panel of the same color. Beginning and ending at the wrist, machine-stitch around the hand and thumb ⅛" from the edge. For a decorative finish, hand-embroider a contrasting blanket stitch (page 117) over the machine stitching, using three strands of floss in a #7 crewel needle.

4. For each mitten, cut an 11" length of dark green satin ribbon. Fold the ribbon in half, tack the midpoint to the plaid ribbon at the center of the wrist, and tie in a bow. Thread each green ribbon tail through a red button, make a knot at the back, and trim off the excess. Fold a 6" length of dark green grosgrain ribbon in half and tack to the inside wrist for a hanging loop (see the template for placement).

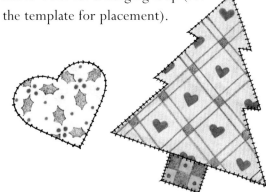

Snowball Wreath

SHOWN ON PAGE 22

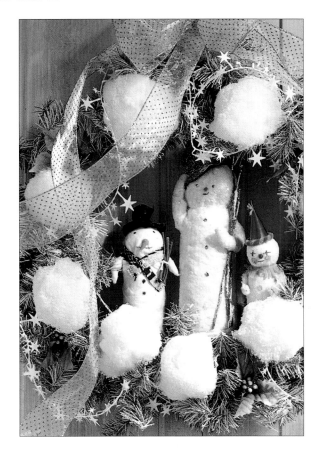

GIVE THE YOUNGSTERS IN YOUR household some fiberfill and assign them the job of making a few snowballs. Nobody's hands will get cold, and you'll all get to enjoy the snowy atmosphere. Before you hang the wreath, you may want to add a bit of fresh greenery behind the top bow, and lightly spray it with white paint to complete the snow effect.

To make one wreath:

20" wire wreath form

Three toy or folk art snowmen, 8" to 14" tall

6' artificial evergreen garland

3 yards white star garland

6 yards 2"-wide white sheer wire-edged ribbon

White snow glitter

Green florist's wire (on paddle)

Fiberfill

Spray adhesive

Hot-glue gun and glue sticks

1. Arrange the artificial evergreen garland on the wire wreath form. Secure it by winding green florist's wire around the form, over and under the concentric rings. When you reach the starting point of the garland, clip the wire from the paddle, then twist and secure the ends.

2. Shape a handful of fiberfill into a ball about 3" in diameter. Don't overwork the shape or try to make it perfectly round—a few lumps and bumps will give the impression of freshly packed snow. Make nine snowballs in all. To avoid sticky fingers, put on rubber gloves. Apply spray adhesive to the balls and roll them in white snow glitter. Hot-glue the snowballs to the wreath.

3. Add the white star garland to the wreath, curling it around the snowballs and passing it back and forth. Tie the sheer white ribbon into a double bow with four streamers. Wire the bow to the top of the wreath and arrange the streamers to flow around it. Stand the three snowmen on the inner rim of the wreath and secure using wire and hot glue.

Egg Cradles

SHOWN ON PAGE 24

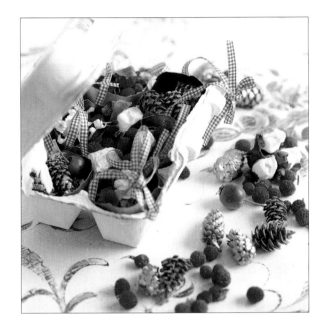

ERE'S AN IMAGINATIVE WAY TO liven up those small potted conifers that are perfect for centerpieces or guest room decor. Each gilded cradle is actually an eggshell, suspended in a ribbon sling. Fill this fairy-tale container with anything tiny that delights the eye. This is a popular idea, so you may want to gather all the elements—packaged in an egg carton, of course—to give as family presents.

To make twenty-four ornaments:

Twelve fresh eggs

Gold spray paint

Assorted natural and purchased fillers, such as fresh or faux cranberries, raspberries, or cherries; gingerbread gnomes or pixie elves; gilded pinecones, acorns, or walnuts; peppermint drops or sourballs; miniature silk roses; tiny twigs and birds' feathers; jingle bells

16 yards ⅜"-wide gingham ribbon

White craft glue

Extra egg cartons

1. Carefully crack the shells in half and reserve the raw eggs for another use. Rinse and dry the empty shells, removing any loose bits of shell. Set the shells in the egg carton compartments and spray-paint the insides gold. When the paint is dry, remove the shells, invert the egg cartons, and stand each shell upside down on one of the carton cups. Spray-paint the outside gold. Let dry overnight.

2. Drape a 24" length of ribbon over each shell, even up the ends, and glue in place. Keep the shells and ribbons in this position until the glue is dry. Turn the shells right side up and set them back in the egg carton compartments. Fill the shells with the fillers, making each shell cradle different. As you are working, lift each shell up by its ribbons to check the balance, and adjust the contents as needed. Tie the egg cradles to your tree with bows.

EGG CRADLE CARRIERS

Give a handmade gift of six or twelve egg cradle ornaments that you've customized for special family friends. For a perfectly witty wrapping, choose paper egg cartons that hold a half dozen or a dozen eggs—you can fill up new ones, but you can often find wonderful vintage cartons (that have never been used) at flea markets and junk shops. Tie cotton rickrack or other trim around each gift carton to keep it closed.

Ribbon Tassels

SHOWN ON PAGE 25

ONCE YOU'VE MADE ONE OF THESE plump ribbon tassels, your head will be brimming with ideas for more. Try pearl beading instead of ribbon roses, or paint your own design on a round wooden bead for the tassel head. Use wire-edged ribbon to achieve plenty of pouf.

To make one tassel:

- 1 yard each ⅜"- to ⅝"-wide sheer ribbons, in four different red and/or green hues (at least three should be wire-edged)
- 1 yard narrow red ribbon rose garland
- 1" satin-covered red ball ornament
- ¼ yard narrow red ribbon, for hanging loop
- Fabric-covered florist's wire
- Hot-glue gun and glue sticks

1. Hold the four wide ribbons together at one end. Run your free hand down all four ribbons to the halfway point. Grip the halfway point firmly and pass it to your other hand, drawing the ribbons up into a circle. Be careful not to twist the ribbon or change the sandwiched order. Repeat the process to make a second loop around the first one. If you find you can't grip both ends of the circle, make it a little smaller. Finish by wrapping the rose garland ribbon once around in the same way; let the excess rose garland hang free.

2. Holding your grip, add the loose part of the circle to the ribbon in your hand, to resemble a two-loop bow. Fold the ribbon in half and bring the groups of loops together to form the bottom of the tassel. Bind the top very tightly with florist's wire.

3. Hot-glue the bound section of the ribbons to the bottom of the satin ball. To ensure a secure join, use plenty of glue and hold the pieces together with your fingers as the glue cools and sets. Wrap the excess rose garland around the join, gluing as you go, to build up a mass of roses at the tassel's head. Hot-glue a narrow ribbon to the top of the ball for a hanging loop. Separate and fluff out the ribbon loops at the bottom of the tassel. Snip the two rose garland loops so the ends dangle free.

TASSEL CHIC

Tassels bring elegance to Christmas—hang them from a door knocker, swing them from a chandelier, tie one onto a special gift wrap, pin one to a stocking, even drape some over the branches of the tree.

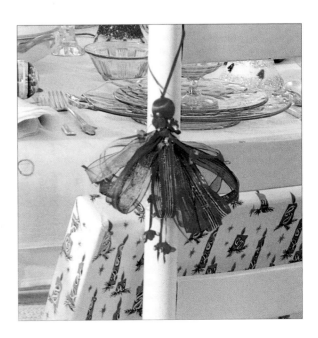

Mitten & Glove Ornaments

SHOWN ON PAGE 26

THE EMBELLISHMENTS ON THESE felt cutouts couldn't be simpler, or sweeter. Re-create the pretty designs with buttons, embroidery floss, and bits of ribbon, or see what your own scrap basket has to offer in the way of inspiration. Felt ornaments like these are favorites of folks who like to decorate with handmade items, because the felt is so durable. Once they're taken from the tree, store them wrapped in tissue paper.

To make three pairs:

Mitten and glove templates (page 136)

9" x 12" felt sheets: 1 red, 1 white

¼ yard ½"-wide red checked ribbon

½ yard ⅜"-wide white satin picot ribbon

Two 1" buttons with white pearls

Four ⅜" white buttons

Pearl cotton: red, white

Red embroidery floss

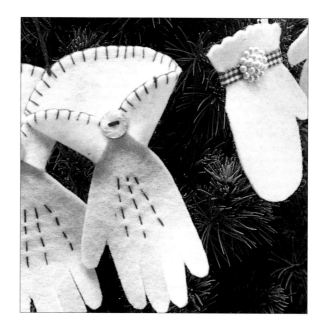

1. Photocopy the templates at 100%, cut them out, and use them to mark two of each mitten and glove on felt. Cut out the pieces just inside the marked outlines so no traces of the marking pencil remain. On each glove, clip in toward the center of the circular cuff, as indicated on the pattern.

2. To assemble the white mittens, fold a 4½" length of checked ribbon around each wrist, overlapping the ends at the middle. Tack through all layers. Sew a white-pearl button to the wrist ribbon to hide the lapped ends. Be sure to reverse the second mitten, so you have a right and a left. Tack one end of the picot ribbon to each mitten for a hanging cord.

3. To assemble the red mittens, arrange a length of white pearl cotton on each wrist edge, looping it as indicated on the pattern. Tack this looped trim in place with white thread. Sew a white button to the center of each mitten. Embroider a French knot (page 117) inside each loop, and work seven French knots around each button. Attach white pearl cotton to each mitten for a hanging cord.

4. To embroider the gloves, use two strands of red floss in a #7 crewel needle. Work a blanket stitch (page 117) around the curved edge of the cuff. Embroider three lines on the face of each glove in straight stitch. Overlap the cuff points and tack them together. Sew on a white button to conceal the stitching. Join the gloves at the cuffs with a length of red pearl cotton for a hanging cord.

Sachet Pillows

SHOWN ON PAGE 27

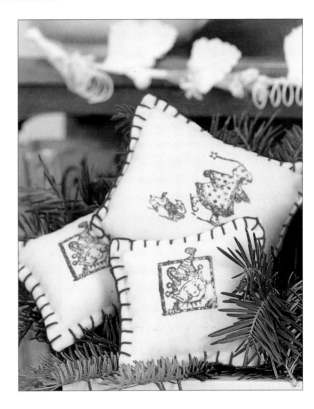

A N OLD LINEN TABLECLOTH IS the perfect fabric source for these tiny pillows. Just cut around yesteryear's gravy stains to get the pieces you need. The pillow dimensions are determined by the rubber stamp image you choose.

To make sachet pillows:

- White linen fabric
- Rubber stamp
- Red opaque pigment stamp pad
- Red embroidery floss
- White monofilament sewing thread
- Fiberfill
- Balsam fir needles

1. Iron the linen fabric smooth and lay it flat on a hard surface. Determine the size pillow you would like and stamp a good, clear image on the fabric, allowing at least a 2" margin all around. Let dry. To mark the pillow outline, measure and mark 1½" beyond the image in each direction. (It's easier to stamp first and then mark, rather than trying to center the stamp precisely in a precut box.)

2. Cut out the stamped pillow front panel on the marked outline. Cut a pillow back panel to match. Place the pieces right sides together and machine-stitch ¼" from the edge all around, leaving a 2" opening for turning. Clip the corners diagonally.

Turn right side out. To create the flange, topstitch ¼" from the edge except at the opening with monofilament thread.

3. Stuff fiberfill into the pillow. Make a nest in the middle and spoon the balsam fir needles into it. Add fiberfill to fill out the edges. Slip-stitch the opening, and complete the flange stitching. Hand-embroider the flange in red blanket stitch (page 117), using 6 strands of floss in a #7 crewel needle.

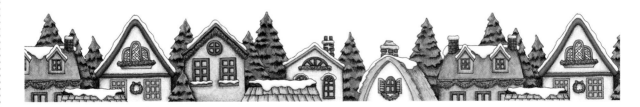

Fondant Snowflakes

SHOWN ON PAGE 38

S UGARY-SWEET FONDANT ROLLS out like cookie dough, ready for cutting out your favorite snowflake or star shapes. If you prefer to use a template, create a folded-paper snowflake with just a few quick scissor snips. The snowflakes also make terrific decorations for a rich Christmas fruitcake that has been draped with a cloak of smooth fondant. You can also give them as greeting cards, slipped into glassine envelopes.

To make eight to twelve snowflakes:

    24 ounces pure white rolled fondant

    .75 ounce tube cake-decorating gel

    Confectioners' sugar

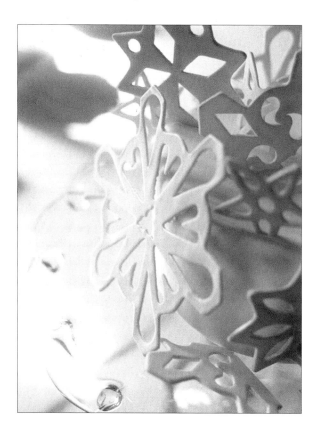

1. To make a snowflake template, cut a square of wax paper to the desired snowflake size, from 4" to 7" across. Fold the square in half and locate the midpoint of the folded edge. Fold the rectangle in thirds by making two creases that radiate from the midpoint. Fold this wedge-shaped piece in half along the midpoint axis. Cut one or two triangles or half-circles along the folded edges. Cut the top edge into a uniform shape. Make the cuts at the broad end of the wedge and keep them simple. Unfold the snowflake and smooth out the creases so the template lies flat.

2. Fondant hardens fairly quickly, so cut off pieces as needed; store the remainder in a resealable plastic bag. You'll need about 3 ounces for a 7" snowflake, 2 ounces for a 5½" to 6" snowflake, and 1 ounce for a 4" snowflake. Dust the work surface and the rolling pin lightly with confectioners' sugar. Roll out the fondant to a ⅛" thickness, rotating or flipping it every few passes to prevent sticking. Use more sugar as needed.

3. Place the snowflake template on top of the rolled-out fondant. Use a paring knife to cut out all the open areas in the template. Start with the smallest cutouts; end by cutting the outside silhouette. Wipe the knife clean on a dry cloth as needed. Gently transfer the snowflake to a sheet of wax paper and let it harden overnight or longer, if necessary. Squeeze cake-decorating gel directly from the tube to write a name or message.

Toy Wreath

SHOWN ON PAGE 49

LITTLE ORNAMENTS AND OLD toys, artfully arranged on a wreath, look as if they just spilled out of Santa's sack. Hot-gluing the pieces is easy, but choosing which toys to include could keep you busy for hours. If you decide to make this wreath with some of your children's outgrown toys, it will become a treasured family memento that your grandchildren will adore.

To make one wreath:

> 14" Styrofoam wreath form
> Eight 4" vintage or reproduction dolls
> 10 to 15 small vintage or reproduction toys
> 6 to 10 small traditional glass ornaments
> 2"-wide black-and-white ribbons:
>> 4½ yards dotted
>> 1¼ yards checked
>> 1¼ yards striped sheer
> Sequin pins
> Hot-glue gun and glue sticks

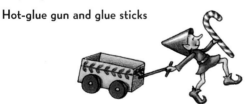

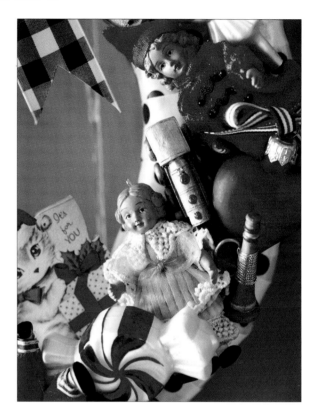

1. Wind the dotted ribbon tightly and evenly around the wreath form, overlapping the ribbon edges so that the form is completely concealed. Secure the ribbon with sequin pins as you go. Tie the checked ribbon into a bow and hot-glue it to the top of the wreath.

2. Lay the wreath flat. Arrange the dolls on the wreath surface, alternating the clothing colors as much as possible. Turn some dolls askew or even upside-down, as if they were tumbling. Add smaller toys to fill the spaces in between. If you have two or more of one toy, set them at different angles. Finally, place the glass ornaments in the remaining blank spaces.

3. Hot-glue the dolls, toys, and ornaments in place one by one. Use generous amounts of glue to ensure a secure hold, but aim the glue gun strategically so that the glue remains hidden. Glue neighboring objects to one another as well as to the wreath where appropriate. To finish, tie the sheer ribbon into a multiloop bow and hot-glue it to the top of the wreath. Notch the ends of the checked ribbon and trim the sheer ribbon ends diagonally.

Scottie Wreath

SHOWN ON PAGE 55

I F ONE SCOTTIE IS NICE, EIGHT are divine. Get the family involved and take an assembly line approach to finish this wreath in an evening or two. These Scotties can be made into endless kinds of decorations—for example, embroider them with names to make placecards.

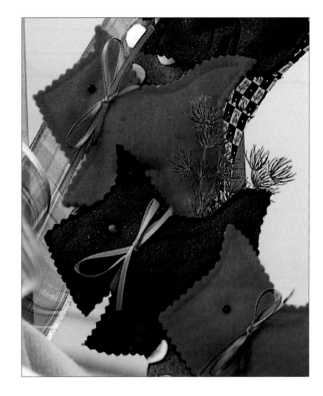

To make one wreath:

Scottie Ornament template (page 137)

13" Styrofoam wreath form

½ yard black-and-white checked fabric

2 yards 2½"-wide sheer plaid wire-edged ribbon

9" x 12" felt sheets: 2 black, 2 red, 2 green, 1 white

2¾ yards ⅛"-wide green double-faced satin ribbon

5mm opaque rocaille beads: 4 black, 4 red

Fiberfill

Hot-glue gun and glue sticks

1. Using pinking shears, cut several 2½"-wide strips from the checked fabric from selvage to selvage. Wrap the strips around the Styrofoam wreath, over-lapping the edges as you go so that the wreath form is completely concealed. Hot-glue the ends in place. Cut more strips as needed.

2. Make eight Scotties—four each in red and black—following the instructions on page 129, steps 1 through 4 (omit hanging loops). Tie a 12" length of green ribbon in a bow around each pup's neck.

3. To make the balls, mark eight 2" circles on a sheet of green felt. Leave space between the markings for cutting. Place two green felt sheets together. Machine-stitch each marked circle through both layers, leaving a 1" opening. Cut out the eight circles with straight-edged scissors ⅛" beyond the stitching line. Stuff lightly with fiberfill and stitch closed. Cut about twenty small white felt dots and hand-sew them to four of the green balls. Stitch narrow white felt strips to the four remaining balls in a tic-tac-toe pattern.

4. Arrange the eight Scotties on the wreath, alternating the colors. Tuck the green balls between, alternating the dot and check patterns. Hot-glue each piece into place. Tie the plaid wire-edged ribbon in a bow and hot-glue it to the top of the wreath. Tuck in sprigs of fresh greenery, if you wish, when displaying the wreath.

Scottie Blanket & Pillow

SHOWN ON PAGE 56

THE WAIT FOR SANTA SEEMS shorter if you're snuggled under a cozy blanket, with your head on a matching pillow. This set is a good companion on a Christmas journey.

To make one blanket and one pillow:

- Scottie Appliqué template (page 137)
- 1 ½ yards 54"-wide black-on-red windowpane plaid wool
- 1 yard 54"-wide black-and-white gingham check wool (⅜" size checks)
- ½ yard 36"-wide black felt
- 15 yards ¼"-wide double-fold bright yellow bias tape
- Fiberfill
- Twenty-two ⁷⁄₁₆" flat black buttons
- Twenty-two ⅝" flat white buttons
- 3¾ yards ⅜"-wide black-and-white checked ribbon
- Twenty-two small silver jingle bells

1. Photocopy the template at 100%, cut it out, and use it to mark 22 Scotties on black felt. Cut out each on the marked outline. Flip over half the felt Scotties so some face left, some right. Sew on a white button topped by a black button for each eye as indicated on the pattern. Set aside a pair of facing Scotties for the pillow.

2. Cut a 36" by 48" piece of windowpane plaid wool. Lay the fabric flat, and place 20 Scottie appliqués on it in five rows. Make the arrangement playful, with neighboring Scotties looking out in different directions. Pin in place. Slip a 6" length of ribbon around each Scottie's neck so the ends meet at the top. Pushing the ribbon aside, machine-stitch around the edges with white thread. Bind the ribbon ends together with thread and tie on a jingle bell. Notch the ends.

3. For the flange, cut the gingham-check fabric into ten strips, from selvage to selvage, using the pattern of the checks as a guide. Make each strip 9 checks across. Sew the strips together end to end, matching the check pattern. Fell the seams. Enclose one long edge in yellow bias tape, following the manufacturer's instructions; allow a 1" excess at each end. To create the ruffles, machine-baste along the long raw edge, folding a single pleat every fourth square.

4. Pin the ruffle around the edge of the blanket, right sides facing and raw edges matching. Allow extra ease at the corners and a 2" overlap where the ends meet. Cut off the excess ruffle and set it aside for the pillow. Machine-stitch a ¼" seam all around, to within 5" of the ruffle ends. Join the ends together, matching the checks and overlapping the bias tape, then complete the blanket/ruffle seam. Fell the seam allowance.

5. For the pillow, cut two 10" by 16" pieces from the windowpane plaid wool. Appliqué the two remaining Scotties to one piece, as in step 2. Sew the remaining ruffle around the edge, as in step 4. Pin the pillow front and back together, right sides facing, making sure the ruffle stays clear of the stitching path. Stitch all around, leaving an opening for turning. Turn right side out. Stuff firmly with fiberfill. Slip-stitch the opening closed.

Scottie Toy

SHOWN ON PAGE 57

TOSS THIS PLUMP SCOTTIE ON the sofa (he makes a perfect neck rest!) or let him guard presents under the tree. His familiar, well-detailed silhouette is actually very easy to achieve—it's cut from black felt. If you're making this for older children, raid the button box to find the perfect eye; for babies and toddlers, forgo the eye for safety's sake.

To make one Scottie:

All four Scottie Toy templates (page 138)
⅜ yard 36"-wide black felt
9" x 12" felt sheets: 1 red, 1 white
¾" flat yellow button
⅝" flat black button
Fiberfill

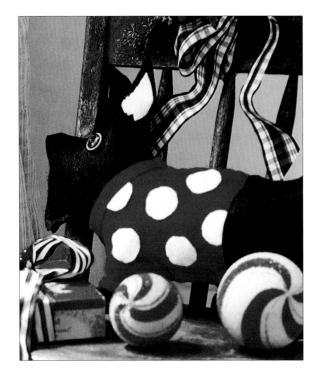

1. Photocopy the templates at 200% and cut out. Cut the black felt in half, and lay one piece on top of the other. Place the template on the felt, and trace the outline with a fabric marking pencil. On the red felt, mark one Scottie sweater. On the white felt, mark six dots and one ear. Cut out the red and white pieces only. Cut just inside the marked outline so no traces of the marking pencil remain.

2. To sew the Scottie, machine-stitch ¼" inside the marked outline through both layers. When you reach an area where the outline becomes jagged, such as the brow or the hind leg and tail, keep the sewing line straight, as indicated on the pattern. Leave a 3" opening along the top edge.

3. Cut out the Scottie just inside the marked outline through both layers. For clean edges, cut into the inside angles from two directions—it's easier than trying to maneuver the scissors out of a tight spot.

4. Position the white ear on the Scottie and hand-sew in place to the top layer of felt only. Stack the black and yellow buttons and sew them in place for an eye, to the top layer only. Insert fiberfill into the opening, being sure to distribute it evenly throughout the Scottie. Poke fiberfill into the animal's feet, tail, and muzzle. (Use a generous amount of fiberfill to create a plump puppy.) Hand-stitch the opening closed.

5. Hand-sew the six white dots to the red sweater. Let one dot overhang the back edge, and trim off the excess. Hand-sew the sweater to the Scottie, folding back the collar and front leg edges as you go. The fit should be snug.

Scottie & Ball Ornaments

SHOWN ON PAGE 59

PINKING SHEARS GIVE THESE Scotties their spunky zigzag edging. The felt shapes are easy to sew—perfect for creative young craftspeople who are just learning how to operate a sewing machine.

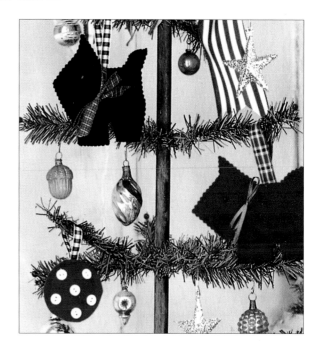

To make two Scotties and two balls:

Scottie Ornament template (page 137)

9" x 12" felt sheets: 1 black, 1 red

¾ yard ⅜"-wide black-and-white checked ribbon

½ yard ⅜"-wide red-and-green plaid ribbon

½ yard ⅜"-wide green ribbon with white dots

5mm opaque rocaille beads: 1 black, 1 red

Twelve white ⅜" buttons

Fiberfill

1. Photocopy the Scottie Ornament template at 100% and cut it out. Cut each felt sheet in half crosswise and lay one piece on top of the other. Place the template on the felt. Trace the outline with a fabric marking pencil. This is your stitching line, so accuracy counts. On the red felt, also mark two 2" circles. Leave ample space between the markings for cutting.

2. Machine-stitch each Scottie along the marked line through both layers of felt. Be sure to leave an opening along the top edge, as shown on the template. When you sew into an angled corner, such as the tip of the tail, stop with the needle sunk down into the felt, lift the presser foot and swivel the felt around to bring the sewing line in the path of the needle, then lower the presser foot and continue sewing.

3. Hand-sew 6 buttons on each of the 2 front panels of the balls. Machine-stitch each circle along the marked line through both layers of red felt, leaving a 1" opening in each.

4. Cut out each Scottie with pinking shears a bit beyond the stitching line all around. Poke some fiberfill into the opening until the Scottie is lightly padded but not bulging. To attach a hanging loop, cut a 7" length of black-and-white checked ribbon. Bring the ends of the ribbon together, insert them into the opening, and stitch the opening closed. Hand-sew a contrasting bead eye to each Scottie. Tie a contrasting ribbon around each Scottie's neck.

5. Cut out each red felt ball with straight-edged scissors. Stuff each circle lightly with fiberfill. Cut a 5" length of ribbon for each hanging loop and attach it as in step 3.

Block Ornaments

SHOWN ON PAGE 79

VINTAGE CHRISTMAS CARDS FROM a flea market, or perhaps your own attic, are your picture source for these decoupaged block ornaments. Look for cards with small, sweet images as well as nicely printed messages. Each block has a light wintry frosting—actually, it's clear glitter.

To make twelve block ornaments:

- Vintage Christmas cards
- Twelve 2" unfinished wooden blocks
- Twelve 3¼" buttons
- 2¾ yards ¼"-wide red ribbon
- Fine clear glitter
- Acrylic craft paints: red, white, ivory
- Gesso (available at arts and crafts stores)
- Decoupage medium
- White craft glue
- 1" and 2" foam brushes
- Small pointed artist's brush
- Medium-grade sandpaper

1. Round off the edges and corners of each block with sandpaper to suggest wear. Sand the flat surfaces to give them some tooth. Using a foam brush, apply a primer coat of gesso to fill in any gaps or nicks and make the surface very smooth. When the gesso is dry, paint the blocks with red or ivory acrylic paint. Let dry.

2. Cut the ribbon into twelve 8" lengths. Thread each ribbon through two button sewing holes and glue the ends together on the underside. Glue a button-and-ribbon hanger to the top of each painted block. Let dry.

3. Select the pictures for your blocks from vintage Christmas cards. Make color photocopies of the pictures on white paper, enlarging or reducing the images as needed to fit within a 2" square. You will need five images per block, or sixty altogether. Try to print multiple pictures on one sheet. Cut the pictures apart with craft scissors. Then use manicure scissors to cut in close to each image and remove all the surrounding white background. (You can also do this close cutting with a craft knife and cutting mat.)

4. Place each cutout facedown on scrap paper. Apply decoupage medium to the back side with a 1" foam brush, going out beyond the edges to ensure full coverage. Position the cutout on one of the blocks and rub gently with your fingertip until it adheres. Check for air bubbles; if you find any, rub gently to coax them out. Blot up any oozing medium around the edges with a moist paper towel. Repeat this process to adhere a picture to all sides and the bottom of each block.

5. Apply the glitter to the blocks one surface at a time. Brush on decoupage medium—go right over the picture, if desired. Sprinkle the glitter evenly across the surface and then tap off the excess. (Use scrap paper to catch and funnel the excess glitter back into its container.) Work assembly line–style, from block to block, and allow each surface to dry before you attempt to coat an adjacent surface. Another embellishment you might try is small polka dots: Load a pointed artist's brush with paint, touch it lightly to the surface, and pull straight up to make a perfectly round dot.

Spot's Stocking

SHOWN ON PAGE 80

EVERY DOG HAS HIS DAY, AND Christmas should be it. For each of your special pets, create a special stocking. Stitch the pooch's name in bold lettering on the top, and you'll get one happy puppy.

To make one stocking:

Stocking template (page 139)

18" x 18" red plaid pinwale corduroy

10" x 13½" red flannel fabric

3" x 14" fabric for name band (see step 4 for more details)

⅞ yard red-and-white striped piping

⅞ yard sage green piping

½ yard dark green tassel fringe

Two ⅝" plaid heart buttons

1. Photocopy the stocking template at 200% and cut it out along the Spot's Stocking cut line. Fold the plaid corduroy fabric in half, right side in. Align the template on the fabric and trace around it with a fabric marking pencil. Cut on the marked line through both layers. With the stockings still layered, machine-stitch all around with a ¼" seam, leaving the top edge open. Hand-baste striped piping around the top opening to the wrong side of the fabric, overlapping the ends. Do not turn.

2. To make the cuff, cut the red flannel in half, into two 5" by 13½" strips. Sew the two strips together along one long edge, enclosing the striped piping and green tassel fringe in the seam (use a zipper foot). Open out the cuff completely. Bring the two shorter edges together, right side in, and stitch a ½"

seam. Trim away the excess bulk and adjust the trims where the two seams meet. Refold the cuff and turn it inside out.

3. Slip the cuff loop around the stocking and align the raw edges and the side seam (use the "heel" side seam on the stocking). Hand-baste all around close to the piping, easing to fit. Machine-baste on the same path with a zipper foot. Turn the stocking right side out and fold down the cuff.

4. Mark the center of the name band fabric with a pin. Measure 2" to the right and left of the pin and 1" above and below it. Use masking tape to mark this 2" by 4" design area. The name can be worked within this area in any media you choose: fabric markers, fabric paint, embroidery, etc. (Pictured on page 80 is 16-count Aida fabric for the name band with a cross-stitched "Spot" done with two strands of sage green floss in a #8 crewel needle.)

5. Fold in the long edges of the name band ½", tuck sage green piping under each fold, and edge-stitch. Test-fit the name band around the stocking cuff, stitch the ends together, and hand-sew in place. Sew the two heart buttons to the name band. Make a hanging loop from the leftover corduroy fabric and tack it in place as indicated on the pattern.

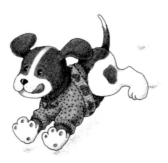

Stocking Collection

SHOWN ON PAGE 82

E ACH ONE'S DIFFERENT, EACH one's special. Pick a stocking for every member of your household. Mix and match the trims, make them long and make them short, and decide which way you'd like the toe to point!

To make one Scottie stocking:

> Stocking, toe pad, and heel pad templates
> (page 139)
> 12" x 20" red felt
> Scrap of black felt
> 1 yard 1⅜"-wide plaid ribbon
> ⅝ yard ⅜"-wide Scottie ribbon
> ⅜ yard black beaded ribbon
> Four 5mm red beads

1. Photocopy the stocking template at 200% and cut it out along the Scottie Stocking cut line. Cut the red felt in half, and lay one piece on top of the other. Place the template on the felt and trace the outline with a fabric marking pencil. Cut on the marked line through both layers. With the stockings still layered, start at the top edge and machine-stitch down the "toe" side for about 4", using a ¼" seam. Open the stocking, right side out.

2. Pin a 12" length of plaid ribbon along the top of the stocking, concealing the cut edge. Slip the beaded ribbon tape under the lower edge of the ribbon. Topstitch through all the layers. Topstitch a 12" length of Scottie ribbon to the middle of the plaid ribbon.

3. Cut the toe and heel pads from black felt. Position them on the stocking front and slipstitch in

place. Refold the stocking right sides together. Continue stitching all around, catching the toe and heel pads and the ribbon trims in the seam. Trim the excess ribbon even with the seam allowance. Turn the stocking right side out.

4. Make a hanging loop from the remaining Scottie ribbon and tack it to the inside top edge. Tack four red beads to the heel pad as indicated on the pattern. Tie the remaining plaid ribbon in a bow and tack it to the ribbon trim on the heel side.

To make one lace-trimmed stocking:

> Stocking and leaf templates (page 139)
> 20" x 20" red midwale corduroy fabric
> White crochet doily, about 5½" diameter
> ⅝ yard ⅝"-wide red-and-white striped grosgrain
>   ribbon
> ¾ yard ⅛"-wide white double-faced satin ribbon
> Scrap of green felt
> 1" unfinished wood disk
> Acrylic craft paints: red, yellow
> Black fine-point permanent marker
> Spray sealer
> Hot-glue gun and glue sticks

1. Photocopy the stocking template at 200% and cut it out along the Lace-Trimmed Stocking cut line. Fold the red corduroy in half along the length-wise grain, right-side in. Align the template on the fabric and trace around it with a fabric marking pencil. Cut on the marked line through both layers. Choose one piece for the stocking front.

2. Cut the doily in half. Position one doily half at the

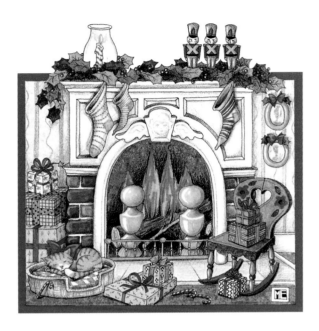

top of the stocking front, aligning the cut edges (see pattern, page 139). Place the other half over the heel. Hand-baste in place. Pin both stockings right sides together. Machine-stitch all around using a ¼" seam, leaving the top edge open. Trim the excess heel doily even with the seam allowance. Machine-overcast the seam allowance to prevent raveling.

3. Turn the stocking right side out. Pin the striped grosgrain ribbon to the wrong side of the open edge, overlapping it about ¼". Machine-stitch the ribbon to the stocking all around. Fold the ribbon onto the right side of the stocking and topstitch through all the layers. Tack the remaining grosgrain ribbon to the top inside corner for a hanging loop.

4. To make the rose, paint a yellow triangle in the middle of the wood disk. Paint the surrounding area red. Draw a few black lines on the red section to suggest overlapping rose petals. Let the paint dry overnight, then apply a spray sealer. Make two felt leaves (see the Cherry Stocking, this page, step 3). Hot-glue the leaves, the painted rose, and three 9" ribbon streamers to the top of the stocking.

To make one cherry stocking:

Stocking and leaf templates (page 139)
20" x 20" red-on-white polka-dot fabric
⅜ yard 2½"-wide candy-cane stripe ribbon
¼ yard ⅝"-wide red-and-white striped
    grosgrain ribbon
12 to 15 plastic cherries with stems
    (see Resources)
Scraps of green felt
Hot-glue gun and glue sticks

1. Photocopy the stocking template at 200% and cut it out along the Cherry Stocking cut line. Fold the polka-dot fabric in half, right side in. Align the template on the fabric; trace around it with a fabric marking pencil. Cut on the line through both layers. With the layers together, start at the top edge and machine-stitch down the "toe" side for 5", using a ¼" seam. Open the stocking. Narrow-hem the top edge.

2. Pin the candy-cane stripe ribbon to the top of the stocking, concealing the overcasting. Topstitch in place. Refold the stocking right sides together and continue stitching all around. Trim the excess ribbon even with the seam allowance. Turn the stocking right side out and lay it face up.

3. Pull the plastic stems off the cherries. Apply a dot of hot glue to the base and tip of each stem and glue it to a red polka dot. Cut a green felt leaf for each stem. To add dimension, fold the leaf in half and press with an iron. Hot-glue one leaf to each plastic stem, varying their placement for a naturalistic look. Tack the grosgrain ribbon to the top inside corner for a hanging loop.

Magazine Cones

SHOWN ON PAGES 84 & 85

NOTHING CONJURES MEMORIES of an old-fashioned Christmas better than the pages of vintage magazines—the holiday issues, of course! Choose pages with recipes, crafts, or advertisements to make a set of easy-to-roll cones. The technique uses color photocopies, which means you can use a favorite image again and again.

To make one cone:

- A Christmas issue of an old magazine
- Card stock
- Assorted rickrack and ribbons
- Vintage or novelty buttons
- Red self-adhesive dots (available at stationery stores)
- Double-sided tape
- Spring-clip clothespin
- Hot-glue gun and glue sticks
- Hole punch (optional)

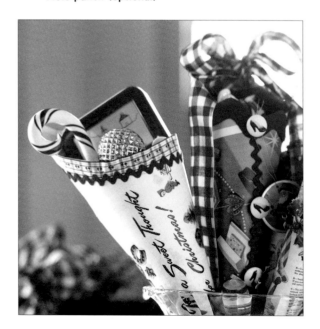

1. Select a page from the magazine for the outside of the cone. To cut the page free, open the magazine flat and run a craft knife along the edge near the spine. Check the image on the reverse side to see if it's appropriate for the inside of the cone. If you'd like something different, find another page, cut it out, and join the two images back to back using double-sided tape. Make a double-sided color photocopy of the sheet on card stock. Trim the card stock to the page size if necessary.

2. Lay the photocopy on a flat surface so the cone's "outside" image faces down. To start the cone, hold down one corner (the bottom of the cone) with your thumb and roll one of the adjacent edges toward the other. At this stage, roll the cone as snug as you can. Lift the cone off the surface, and allow it to relax and open up a bit. Maneuver the twist so that the crisscrossed edges fall at the front, in line with the cone's top point. Once the desired shape is reached, temporarily secure the crisscrossed edges with a clothespin. Hot-glue all the outer edges.

3. Select ribbons and rickrack to accentuate the cone opening (try jumbo rickrack), to camouflage a seam, or simply as a decoration. Do a dry run first, without glue, to try out different combinations and plan where you'll hide the ends. Don't cut the trims until after they are glued—longer lengths are easier to work with, and there's less risk of burning your fingers. When you're ready, apply the hot glue a few inches at a time, press the trim in place, and repeat. You can also glue on buttons or apply self-adhesive polka dots. To hang, punch two holes below the top point and thread with a decorative ribbon.

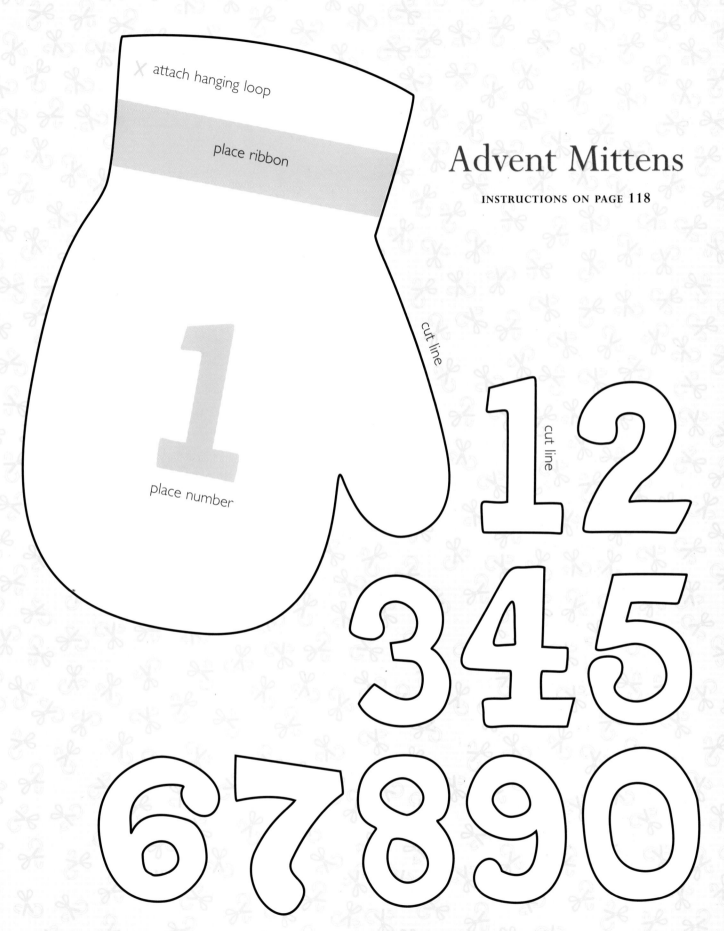

attach hanging loop

place ribbon

1

place number

Advent Mittens

INSTRUCTIONS ON PAGE 118

cut line

cut line

12
345
67890

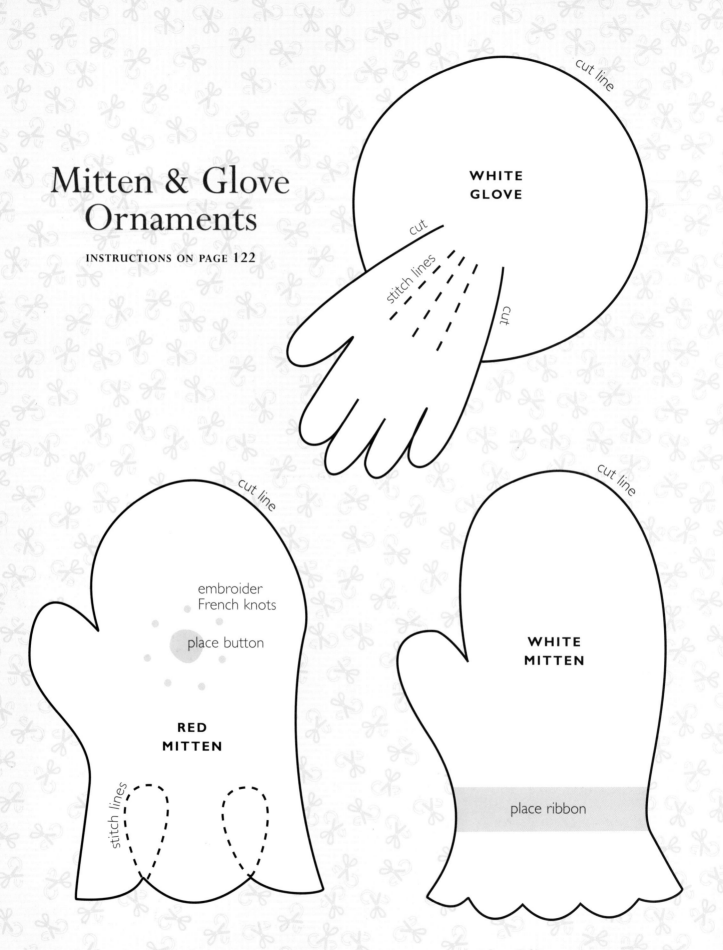

Mitten & Glove Ornaments

INSTRUCTIONS ON PAGE 122

WHITE GLOVE

cut line

cut

stitch lines

cut

RED MITTEN

cut line

embroider French knots

place button

stitch lines

WHITE MITTEN

cut line

place ribbon

Scottie Appliqué

INSTRUCTIONS ON PAGE 127

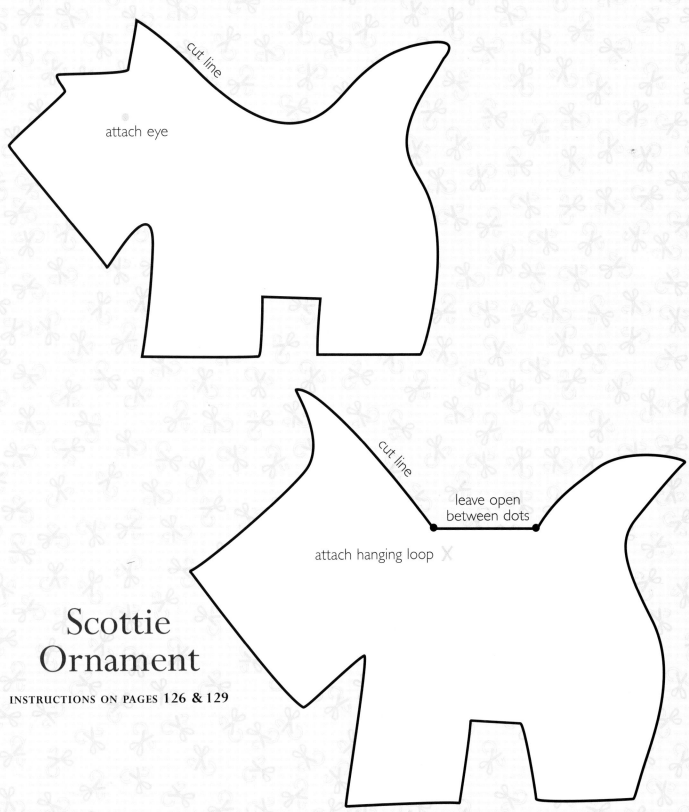

cut line

attach eye

cut line

leave open
between dots

attach hanging loop X

Scottie
Ornament

INSTRUCTIONS ON PAGES 126 & 129

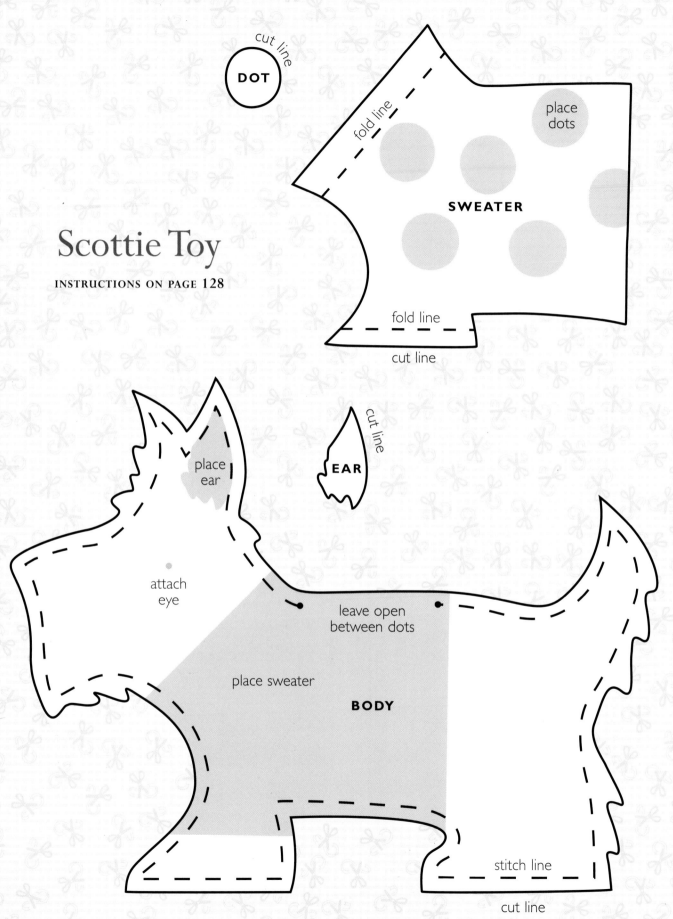

cut line

DOT

place
dots

fold line

SWEATER

fold line

cut line

Scottie Toy

INSTRUCTIONS ON PAGE 128

cut line

place
ear

EAR

attach
eye

leave open
between dots

place sweater

BODY

stitch line

cut line

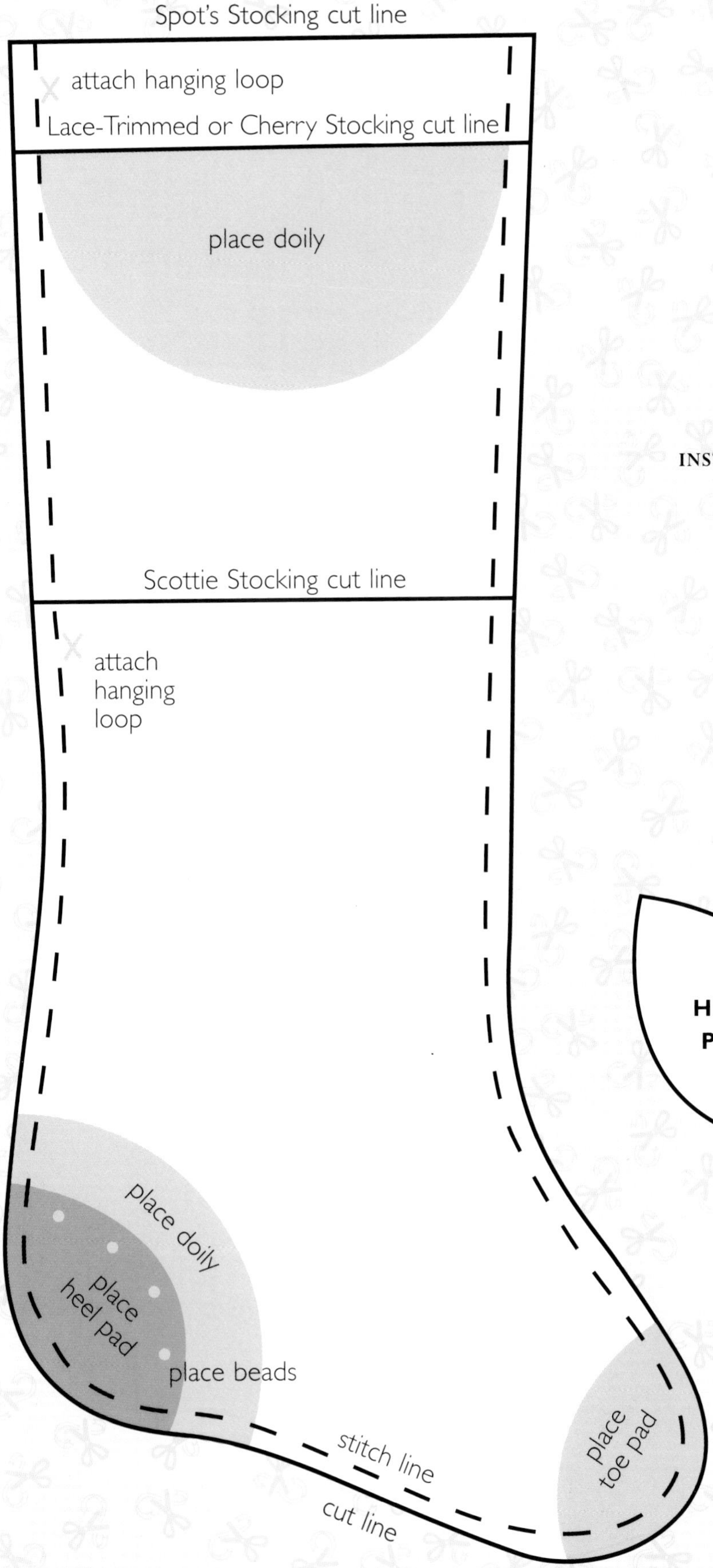

Spot's Stocking cut line

attach hanging loop

Lace-Trimmed or Cherry Stocking cut line

place doily

Scottie Stocking cut line

attach
hanging
loop

Stockings

INSTRUCTIONS ON PAGES 131–133

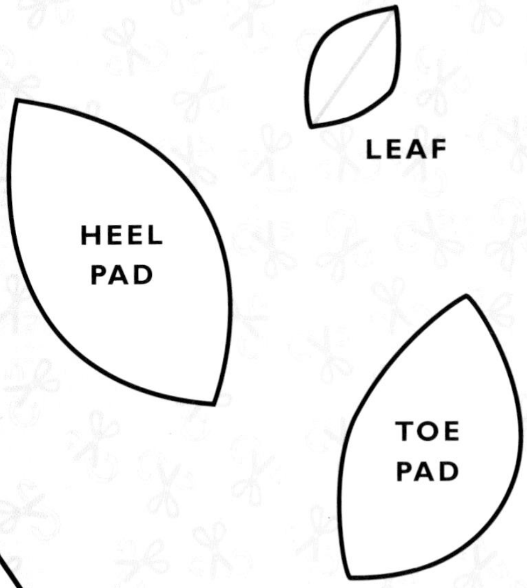

LEAF

HEEL
PAD

place doily

place
heel pad

place beads

stitch line

cut line

TOE
PAD

Place
toe pad

RESOURCES

Be Warm Inside & Out

PAGE 15
Buffet from Ken Miesner's, 292 Plaza Frontenac, St. Louis, MO 63131; (314) 567-6650

PAGE 18
Ribbon from Mokuba, 55 West 39th Street, New York, NY 10018; (212) 869-8900

PAGE 23
Ribbon from Midori Inc., (800) 659-3049; www.midoriribbon.com

PAGE 24
Tree from Sugar Hill Wreaths, (800) 572-0488

PAGE 25
Ribbon from Offray, www.offray.com

PAGE 26
Tree from Sugar Hill Wreaths, (800) 572-0488

PAGE 29
Silver trees from Midwest of Cannon Falls, (800) 776-2075; www.midwestofcannonfalls.com

PAGE 30
Tables and chairs from Jane Keltner Designs, (800) 487-8033; www.janekeltner.com

Twig sideboard from Willows At Home, (580) 420-3735; willows@pine-net.com

PAGE 31
Gold mirror from Thomas W. McCanna, Rebus Eye Studio, 5 Somerset Road, Provincetown, MA 02657; (508) 487-6474

PAGE 34
Holly mints from Reva Paul Christmas Sugar Mints, (212) 722-0486

PAGE 39
Pastries from Mondo, 750 Huff Road NW, Atlanta, GA 30318; (404) 603-9995

Three-tiered cake stand by Groundwork, available from Relish, (404) 355-3735

Handmade snowman from Christy Silacci, (707) 795-0462; csilacci@sonic.net

Antique furniture from Darva Murray, (404) 853-5065

Ribbon from Midori Inc., (800) 659-3049; www.midoriribbon.com

Scotties & Checks

PAGE 42
Plastic cherries from Mary Engelbreit, (314) 863-5522

PAGE 44
Vintage tin toys from Second Childhood, 283 Bleecker Street, New York, NY 10014; (212) 989-6140 and from Bill Bertoia Auctions, 1889 S. Spring Road, Vineland, NJ 08361; (865) 692-1881

PAGE 45
Pastel-colored glass ornaments from Neiman Marcus, www.neimanmarcus.com

PAGE 49
Reproduction vintage toys and ornaments from Midwest of Cannon Falls, (800) 776-2075; www.midwestofcannonfalls.com

Ribbon from Offray, www.offray.com

PAGES 50 & 51
Ribbon from Mokuba, 55 West 39th Street, New York, NY 10018; (212) 869-8900

Comfort & Joy

Crafts

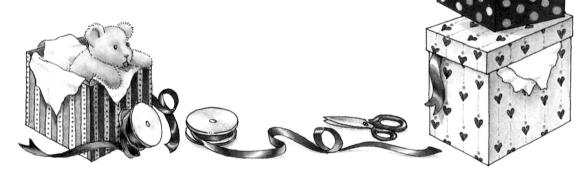

PLEASE JOIN US

For information about **Mary Engelbreit** stores, contact our store in St. Louis at **Saint Louis Galleria, 1142 Saint Louis Galleria, St. Louis, MO 63117**; (314) 863-5522. To subscribe to *Mary Engelbreit's Home Companion* magazine, call us toll-free at (800) 826-3382. You can always visit us online at www.maryengelbreit.com.

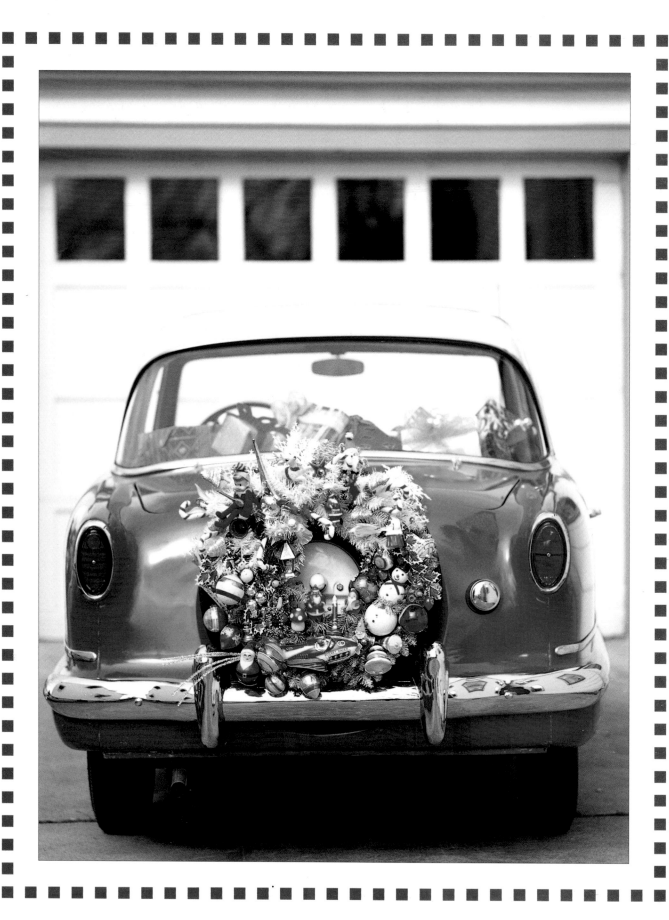